Jesus on ThyFace

Social Networking for the Modern Messiah

Denise Haskew and Steve W Parker
(based on an original idea by Jesus)

 Virgin Mary I once met the Archangel
Gabriel, you know. He said I was going to
have a son by the Holy Ghost and I should
call him Emmanuel. But Joseph said that
was a girl's name, and a bit slutty, so we
settled on Jesus.
🕐 Tuesday 1 March 29AD at 10:00am

SIMON &
SCHUSTER

First published in Great Britain by Simon & Schuster UK Ltd, 2010
A CBS Company

1 3 5 7 9 10 8 6 4 2

Simon & Schuster UK Ltd
1st Floor
222 Gray's Inn Road
London
WC1X 8HB

www.simonandschuster.co.uk

Simon & Schuster Australia
Sydney

A CIP catalogue for this book is available
from the British Library.

ISBN: 978-0-85720-145-4

Printed and bound in Spain by Graficas Estella

*I dedicate this book to my Father,
without whom – well, everything really…*

Special introduction by Jesus Christ

Some years ago, several short biographies of my life were published in an anthology of works you may or may not have come across called "The Bible", which, without blowing my Angels' trumpets, went on to become the best-selling book of all time. Although laudable in many ways, I always felt these biographies lacked the immediacy of the actual events, as well as being somewhat light on laughs, and for some time I toyed with the idea of submitting my own version to a publisher for their consideration.

Of course, there are many other people whose stories are interwoven with mine: my cousins, the Zebedees, John the Baptist, my mum (the Virgin Mary), not to mention Pontius Pilate, the Roman Governor at the time. Then it struck me – we were all mad crazy on social networking back then, and everyone had a ThyFace account. So I thought, what could be more immediate than reading my story as it unfolded on our ThyFace scrolls? So I contacted the guys – most of them are up here anyway, although a few of them are living in "another place", shall we say. And I'm glad to report, they all gave their immediate blessing.

So here it is: the story of the last four years of my time on Earth as revealed on ThyFace, the forerunner of modern social networking sites such as MySpace and Facebook.

Blessed art thou. Amen

Jesus Christ

Jesus of Nazareth, Christ, Messiah, Son of God, Son of Man, ecce homo, Light of the World, Lamb of God, King of Kings, &c.

v

THY-FACE.COM
COMMANDMENTS OF USE

I   THOU SHALT NOT POST ANYTHING DISCRIMINATORY ON THYFACE, EXCEPT IT BE DIRECTED AGAINST WOMEN, GENTILES OR HOMOS.

II   THOU SHALT NOT ADVERTISE SLAVES OR OTHER LIVESTOCK ON THYFACE WITHOUT PERMISSION.

III   THOU SHALT NOT ENGAGE IN PYRAMID SCHEMES OR OTHER DUBIOUS EGYPTIAN BUILDING PROJECTS.

IV   THOU SHALT NOT UPLOAD PLAGUES.

V   THOU SHALT NOT BULLY, INTIMIDATE OR HARASS OTHER USERS (ROMANS EXEMPT BY ARRANGEMENT).

VI   THOU SHALT NOT POST CONTENT THAT IS WRATHFUL, MALICIOUS OR HATEFUL, EXCEPT IN THAT THOU ART QUOTING THE SCRIPTURES.

VII   THOU SHALT NOT POST CONTENT OF A GRAPHIC SEXUAL NATURE OTHER THAN OF SLAVES OR CAMELS.

VIII   THOU SHALT NOT UPLOAD SCENES OF GRAPHIC OR GRATUITOUS VIOLENCE EXCEPTING IT BE RELIGIOUSLY SANCTIONED TORTURE OR PUNISHMENT.

IX   THOU SHALT NOT ALLOW OTHER PEOPLE TO SIT ON THYFACE UNLESS THOU ART IN A DEEPLY COMMITTED RELATIONSHIP.

X   THOU SHALT NOT SMITE THE WRITERS, EDITORS OR PUBLISHERS OF JESUS ON THYFACE, BUT THOU ART WELCOME TO PURCHASE ADDITIONAL COPIES FOR THE PURPOSE OF PROTEST BURNING.

WARNING: IT HATH COME TO OUR ATTENTION THAT WOMEN HATH BEEN USING THYFACE WITHOUT THE PERMISSION OF THEIR HUSBAND OR FATHER AND THUS MAY BE PROCLAIMING VIEWS NOT SANCTIONED BY THEIR MENFOLK. WE ART SORROWFUL FOR THIS OVERSIGHT AND SHALT WORK ON TIGHTENING SECURITY IN THE NEXT VERSION OF THE SOFTWARE.

THY-FACE.COM

Jesus Christ

What's on thy mind?

HATH COME TO PASS

😊 Jesus Christ joined ThyFace.

❗ Jesus Christ and James Zebedee are now friends. • Saith • Liketh

❗ Jesus Christ and John Zebedee are now friends. • Saith • Liketh

⊘ Jesus Christ rejected a friend request from Jesus H Christ. • Saith • Liketh

Welcome to ThyFace, the friendly, laid-back social networking community that helps you keep in touch with your pals. Please take a moment to review our few short rules, as failure to comply with these could lead to summary execution and your family being sold into slavery for up to six years.

HATH COME TO PASS

❗ Jesus Christ and Virgin Mary are now friends. • Saith • Liketh

⊘ Jesus Christ declined the event Stoning of Philip the Samaritan.

 Virgin Mary I was tidying out the stable and came across these icons. Don't you look cute!!!? I do love Bethlehem, but it wasn't the best place for kiddies back then, particularly the under-twos.

🕐 Tuesday 1 March 29AD at 4:16pm • Comment • Liketh

 Jesus Christ How do you stop someone posting on your scroll?

🕐 Tuesday 1 March 29AD at 4:19pm • Saith • Liketh

 John Zebedee Awesome icons, dude! Love the one of the seagull evacuating on your head! lol!
🕐 Tuesday 1 March 29AD at 4:22pm

HATH COME TO PASS

🍀 Jesus Christ joined the group I Was Born In A Stable. • Saith • Liketh

View Mine Icons (4)

Edit Mine Profile

Humble carpenter

Personal Information

Birthday
25 December

Status
Holy Trinity

Website:
/www.goodwithwood.il

Proclamations

John the Baptist live!

He lives alone in the Wilderness on locusts and wild honey. And he's baptising in the River Jordan for five days only. Book now!

👍 Liketh 👎 Despiseth

Cartoon thyself!

Turn yourself into a cartoon and post it on your ThyFace profile.

👍 Liketh 👎 Despiseth

Loggeth out

Friends
Jesus Christ hath 3 friends
See all
Find more friends

John Zebedee   Virgin Mary   James Zebedee

Crispy locust and wild honey fricassee

Add to thy favourites

You will need a good quart of fresh locusts for this recipe, and the olive oil has to be piping hot, otherwise the heads won't be crispy.

If fresh locusts aren't available, any insect or arthropod will do. I often substitute bluebottles.

Ingredients
36 locusts (fresh)
1 cup wild honey
1 tbsp olive oil
½ tsp thyme
3 large tomatoes
pinch of salt
dash of balsamic vinegar (opt)

Preparation
Prepare the locusts by parching them over an open fire until their wings and legs fall off. Reserve for the gravy. When heads and backs are bright red, and screaming subsides to barely audible level, set aside.

Cooking
Meanwhile, heat the oil in a heavy-bottomed pan over a high heat. Add the locusts and fry for three minutes. Remove and set aside. Add the tomatoes, thyme and salt to the >MORE

If you enjoyed this recipe, why not try one of these?

Crunchy Coupling Locust Salad

Camel Spider Thermidor

Baby Arachnid Orange Cup Cakes

THY-FACE.COM

John the Baptist

HATH COME TO PASS

 John the Baptist joined the group Cooking With Locusts. • Saith • Liketh

 John the Baptist and Jesus Christ are now friends. • Saith • Liketh

223 more similar stories

 John the Baptist Repent ye: for the kingdom of heaven is at hand!

🕐 Monday 7 March 29AD at 11:00am. • Saith • Liketh

> **Herod Philip** Art thou the Messiah?
> 🕐 Monday 7 March 29AD at 11:14am

> **John the Baptist** Nay.
> 🕐 Monday 7 March 29AD at 11:15am

> **John Zebedee** Art thou a horse!?
> 🕐 Monday 7 March 29AD at 12:02pm

> **John the Baptist** I've warned thee!!
> 🕐 Monday 7 March 29AD at 12:03pm

> **Joseph ben Caiaphas** Who the hell art thou then?
> 🕐 Monday 7 March 29AD at 12:05pm

 John the Baptist I am the messenger who hath come first to prepare the way for the one who cometh after me. For there shall come one mightier than I, after me, and I shall precede him, the one who followeth after me, and the latchet of his shoes I am not worthy to stoop down and unloose.

🕐 Monday 7 March 29AD at 12:07pm • Saith • Liketh

 Jesus Christ Hi, do I have to make an appointment, or should I just come along?

🕐 Monday 7 March 29AD at 2:12pm • Saith • Liketh

 John the Baptist Behold! The lamb of God!

🕐 Monday 7 March 29AD at 2:13pm • Saith • Liketh

> **John Zebedee** I thought it was a baptism not a baa-mitzvah!!!
> 🕐 Monday 7 March 29AD at 2:16pm

> **James Zebedee** Watch out! He'll baa you!! lol!
> 🕐 Monday 7 March 29AD at 2:18pm

HATH COME TO PASS

🚫 John the Baptist hath blocked John Zebedee and James Zebedee.

Friends
John the Baptist hath 1016 friends
See all
Find more friends

 Joseph b Caiaphas   Herod Philip   No image Prophet Muhammad   Jesus Christ

Amenities

Guide to The Wilderness

Restaurants
None

Bars
None

Hotels
None

Places of interest
None

Entertainment
None

Best time to visit
Never

Map of The Wilderness

← **Civilisation**

Scale 1:10000

THY-FACE.COM

Jesus Christ

HATH COME TO PASS

 Jesus Christ joined the ThyFace group Magi Circle. • Saith • Liketh

Jesus Christ and Andrew the Fish are now friends. • Saith • Liketh

Jesus Christ and Herod Philip are now friends. • Saith • Liketh

176 more similar stories

 Jesus Christ What a day! Went to get baptised by John the Baptist, but when I got there, JB wanted me to baptise him! It was so funny! Finally, we agreed to baptise each other, but then we couldn't decide who was going to go first and we ended up bowing down at the same time and bashing heads!! Everyone thought it was hilarious!

⏰ Tuesday 8 March 29AD at 5:53pm. • Saith • Liketh

> John Zebedee Do you have any idea how gay that sounds?
> ⏰ Tuesday 8 March 29AD at 5:56pm

> James Zebedee And you rounded it off by towel-flicking each other in the showers!
> ⏰ Tuesday 8 March 29AD at 5:57pm

> Virgin Mary Well, I'm glad the swimming lessons came in handy.
> ⏰ Tuesday 8 March 29AD at 6:05pm

> John Zebedee lol
> ⏰ Tuesday 8 March 29AD at 6:05pm

HATH COME TO PASS

Jesus Christ and The Holy Ghost are now friends. • Saith • Liketh

 Jesus Christ I'm off fasting in the Wilderness tomorrow. I'm embarking on my ministry soon, and I have to sort out my head first. I did think my mates would be a bit more flipping supportive!

⏰ Tuesday 8 March 29AD at 7:16pm • Saith • Liketh

> Virgin Mary Jesus! Language! Anyway, come round in the morning and I'll make you some sandwiches to take with you.
> ⏰ Tuesday 8 March 29AD at 7:18pm

 The Holy Ghost I fink you done good. Well, done, my son! I'm well pleased!

⏰ Tuesday 8 March 29AD at 7:21pm • Saith • Liketh

View Mine Icons (4)

Edit Mine Profile

The Lamb of God

Personal Information

Status: **Single** Dwelleth: **Nazareth**

Website: **www.goodwithwood.il**

Proclamations

Plague insurance

Covers locusts, flies, boils, hail, frogs, lice and death of the first-born*. **Temple Moneychangers.** The insurer that cares.

* excludes Acts of God

👍 Liketh 👎 Despiseth

Rate this hottie!!!

👍 Liketh 👎 Despiseth

Loggeth out

Friends
Jesus Christ hath 183 friends
See all
Find more friends

 Virgin Mary John the Baptist Simon Zelotes Herod Philip

HELL-O!

THE EMPEROR ON HOLIDAY
TIBERIUS AND PALS LIVE IT UP ON THE ISLAND OF CAPRI

UNDERWORLD EXCLUSIVE

RELAXING AT HIS OWN NIGHTCLUB

PRINCE SATAN OF DARKNESS

HIS MOST REVEALING INTERVIEW YET

- THE TRUTH ABOUT RICHARD DAWKINS AND ME
- WHY I JUST CAN'T GET ENOUGH SHOES

PRINCESS SALOME
TALKING BOYS AND BURLESQUE DANCING

PLUS: CELEBRITIES GIVE US THEIR TOP SECRET FASTING TIPS

HERODIAS EXCLUSIVE
MARRIAGE TO HEROD PHILIP 'ON THE ROCKS' SAY FRIENDS

HAVING A DEVIL OF A TIME WITH SATAN

We met in an underground nightclub and casino called Dante's Inferno. Satan was waiting at the bar, nursing a long cocktail called Blood of the Martyrs, which he had apparently concocted himself. It looked a bit dangerous for my tastes, so I opted for a martini on the rocks. Satan explained that he had bought the club some years before as a hang-out for him and his minions. There just weren't any places that shared his musical and cultural tastes, so he created his own. "You won't find any Cliff Richard on the juke box," he quipped.

It was a quiet night. "Sabbath nights are usually the quietest," he explained. "We used to have a quiz, but we kept losing the quiz masters. Our clientele tend to get a bit upset when they lose." Satan chuckled loudly at this, betraying a habit of laughing maniacally at his own comments, which can be a little unsettling. As always, the Prince of Darkness was extremely well turned-out in a fawn suit and snakeskin brogues. When I commented on his shoes, he told me they were made from his own skin which he had shed in the Garden of Eden back in the ▶

XII

THY-FACE.COM

Satan

HATH COME TO PASS

✍ Satan took the ThyFace test Which Friends Character Are You Most Like? Satan is most like Rachel. • Saith • Liketh

! Satan and Jesus Christ are now friends. • Saith • Liketh

! Satan and Philip Pullman are now friends. • Saith • Liketh

176 more similar stories

 Jesus Christ Well, I've been in the Wilderness for what seems like ages, and this is the first time I've been able to get online. There are a couple of camel drivers down in the valley and they must have an unsecured network. Have to say I'm absolutely famished.
⏱ Sunday 17 April 29AD at 1:30pm • Saith • Liketh

 Satan Hey Jesus, you're right above my club. Why don't you pop down for a Bloody Mary? We have a top chef – brought him all the way from Gaul. You should see what he can do with a loaf of unleavened bread!
⏱ Sunday 17 April 29AD at 1:32pm • Saith • Liketh

> Jesus Christ Man cannot live on bread alone.
> ⏱ Sunday 17 April 29AD at 1:33pm

> Satan Then you should take in a lodger! Ha-ha, ha-ha. No, but seriously, if you're lonely, I can provide you with company. You haven't been anointed till you've been anointed by one of my girls!
> ⏱ Sunday 17 April 29AD at 1:36pm

> Jesus Christ I'm sorry, but that doesn't appeal to me.
> ⏱ Sunday 17 April 29AD at 1:38pm

> Satan Well, why didn't you say so? If you prefer a bit of Greek, we're very broad-minded down here. We have to be since the Romans tipped up! He who pays the piper gets his pipe played, as we say!
> ⏱ Sunday 17 April 29AD at 1:41pm

> Jesus Christ You are a thoroughly bad person.
> ⏱ Sunday 17 April 29AD at 1:42pm

> Satan Why, thank you. Oh, I get it. Stable boy! We have a tremendous petting zoo round the back.
> ⏱ Sunday 17 April 29AD at 1:45pm

HATH COME TO PASS

⊘ Jesus Christ hath blocked Satan. • Saith • Liketh

View Mine Icons (69)

Edit Mine Profile

Mad, bad and easy on the eye

Personal Information

Status	Dwelleth
Fallen	**7th Circle of Hell**

Website:
www.abandonallhope.fr

Loggeth out

Friends
Satan hath 666 friends
See all
Find more friends

| Gaius Caligula | Adolf Hitler | L Ron Hubbard | Genghis Khan |

THY-FACE.COM

Jesus Christ

 Jesus Christ posted these icons of the Wilderness.

🕐 Tuesday 18 April 29AD at 4:04pm • Saith • Liketh

 James Zebedee Be sure to book early for next year!
🕐 Tuesday 18 April 29AD at 4:05pm

HATH COME TO PASS

 Jesus Christ formed the group Born Again in Me. • Saith • Liketh

 Joseph of Arimathea joined the group Born Again in Me. • Saith • Liketh

 Nicodemus ben Gurion joined the group Born Again in Me. • Saith • Liketh

510 similar stories

 Andrew the Fish Hi Jesus. We haven't met, but I'm a follower of John the Baptist. Well, I say follower: I help out with the catering at his baptism bashes. Deal with the fish, mainly. That's my line (if you'll excuse the pun!) – fish. You might have seen my ads? Andrew the Fish: The Perfect Dish? No matter. Anyway, JB mentioned you were about to embark on a tour. Would it be OK if I popped by to introduce myself? I have my own donkey.
🕐 Friday 12 May 29AD at 3:00pm • Saith • Liketh

Jesus Christ I recognise you from the baptism. You were standing next to the aesthetically challenged bloke who looked a bit like a bouncer.
🕐 Friday 12 May 29AD at 3:00pm

Andrew the Fish Yes, that's my brother Simon.
🕐 Friday 12 May 29AD at 3:07pm

Jesus Christ Then I shall call him Peter, which is "aesthetically challenged bloke". Bring him along.
🕐 Friday 12 May 29AD at 3:10pm

View Mine Icons (8)

Edit Mine Profile

Be Born Again!

Personal Information

Status — **Single**

Dwelleth — **Wilderness**

Website:
www.goodwithwood.il

Proclamations

Loggeth out

Friends
Jesus Christ hath 262 friends
See all
Find more friends

 James Zebedee
 Satan
 Andrew the Fish
 Humpy Pumpy

begat.com
who doth thou think thou art?

begat.com hath traced the genealogy of Herod Philip

XVI

THY-FACE.COM

Jesus Christ

 Herod Philip art sorrowful.
🕐 Friday 24 June 29AD at 12:14pm • Saith • Liketh

 Jesus Christ art sorrowful on Herod Philip's behalf. What's wrong, Herod Philip?
🕐 Friday 24 June 29AD at 12:15pm • Saith • Liketh

> Herod Philip My wife Herodias hath left me, and taken my daughter Salome with her.
> 🕐 Friday 24 June 29AD at 12:16pm

> John the Baptist That brazen harlot strumpet! Satan hath taken your wife and doth indulge his vile and perverted lust on her! She and the devil doth couple in carnal sin and make the very Earth a bed for wanton caresses and unnatural rutting!
> 🕐 Friday 24 June 29AD at 12:17pm

> John Zebedee is feeling horny!!!
> 🕐 Friday 24 June 29AD at 12:18pm

> Herod Philip Actually, she's run off with Antipas.
> 🕐 Friday 24 June 29AD at 12:19pm

> James Zebedee Woah, dude! Let's get this straight. You marry your own niece, then she dumps you for your brother? Your family tree must be horizontal!
> 🕐 Friday 24 June 29AD at 12:20pm

> John Zebedee Don't worry, Philip, you'll find love again. I hear your granny's still single! lol!
> 🕐 Friday 24 June 29AD at 12:21pm

> John the Baptist The Whore of Babylon doth couple with the Beast of the Apocalypse, and the strumpet Herodias doth proffer nipples that drippeth with the blood of Israel, and Herod Antipas doth commit sodomy in the Temple and fornicate with her to the baying of nine hundred tiny demons. And they shall burn for all eternity in the fiery pits of Hell for their wretched adultery!!
> 🕐 Friday 24 June 29AD at 12:24pm

> John Zebedee Dude, seriously, get a girlfriend.
> 🕐 Friday 24 June 29AD at 12:25pm

 Jesus Christ Herod Antipas has arrested John the Baptist! You know what, I think about it I might start my ministry in Samaria.
🕐 Friday 24 June 29AD at 5:13pm • Saith • Liketh

View Mine Icons (9)
Edit Mine Profile

Marriage Guidance Counsellor

Personal Information

Star sign | Status
Capricorn | **Single**

Website:
www.bornagaininme.il

Proclamations

THYFACE **emoticons**

Let your friends know your mood without using boring words. Why not try the following:
- 😊 I art joyful…
- ☹ I art sorrowful…
- 🗲 I'd like to smite…
- ♥ I doth adore…
- 😠 I doth despise…
- ✝ I'd like to crucify…

👍 Liketh   💬 Despiseth

Goat-Compare.com

We compare loads of insurance quotes and bring you great deals on goats, sheep, camels and oxen.

👍 Liketh   💬 Despiseth

Loggeth out

Friends
Jesus Christ hath 1641 friends
See all
Find more friends

 Simon Peter   Angel Gabriel   Holy Ghost   John the Baptist

Janus & Janus
Rome's Leading Pharmaceutical Company

Dear Mr Christ

We have recently been made aware of some alleged successes you have enjoyed in the treatment of the condition known by the medical professional as leprosy, or as it is referred to by the Roman man in the streets: mycobacterium lepromatosis.

Janus & Janus is the leading research company in this field and we would be interested in an initial exploratory meeting with you about potential areas of medical synergy. We enjoy excellent research facilities as well as the funds to patent any treatments we develop. We may be in a position to offer you a one-off payment for the rights to any medical breakthrough you may have made, as well as other gifts at our disposal. We do for instance sponsor the University of Damascus (previously South Syrian College of Further Education), and off-the-record may be in a position to arrange the conferal of an honorary doctorate.

That being said, we must warn you that if you are using healing techniques not developed by yourself, you may inadvertently be in breach of one of our patents. Thus, I would urge you to contact me to arrange a meeting at the earliest opportunity.

Yours

ML

Marcus Lexus
Senior attorney
Janus & Janus

THY-FACE.COM

Jesus Christ

 Simon the Leper Jesus. I'd just like to thank you again for curing my leprosy. I've taken the liberty of attaching an icon of the event.

⏱ Wednesday 31 May 30AD at 12:01pm • Saith • Liketh

HATH COME TO PASS

❗ Jesus Christ and Derek the Leper are now friends. • Saith • Liketh

❗ Jesus Christ and Geoffrey the Leper are now friends. • Saith • Liketh

11,433 similar stories

 Simon Peter Do we have to do so much healing? What's wrong with just preaching once in a while?

⏱ Wednesday 31 May 30AD at 6:14pm • Saith • Liketh

 Jesus Christ I'm surprised at you, Peter. Especially after I healed your mother-in-law. How is she now?

⏱ Wednesday 31 May 30AD at 6:18pm

 Simon Peter Don't ask! Morning, noon and night it's "how's that nice Jesus?" "Why can't you be more like Jesus?" "Jesus wouldn't talk to his mother-in-law like that" "Why can't you catch more fish? I bet Jesus could catch more fish". Seriously, can't you give her laryngitis?

⏱ Wednesday 31 May 30AD at 6:20pm

 Matthew Levi You all coming round mine this Sabbath? We can swig some jars and do a bit of healing.

⏱ Thursday 1 June 30AD at 10:14am • Saith • Liketh

 John Zebedee Yeah, if anyone moans about us healing on the Sabbath again, we'll tell them the Holy Day has been changed from Saturday to Sunday. These people will believe anything!

⏱ Thursday 1 June 30AD at 10:16am.

HATH COME TO PASS

✉ Jesus Christ agreed to attend the event Marriage at Cana. • Saith • Liketh

---

View Mine Icons (9)

Edit Mine Profile

Medical student

Personal Information

Birthday	Dwelleth
25 December	**Bethsaida**

Website:
www.bornagaininme.il

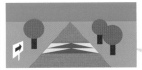

Loggeth out

Friends
Jesus Christ hath 17889 friends
See all
Find more friends

| Simon the Leper | Susanna Myrbarer | Simon Peter | John Zebedee |

WEDDING GIFT LIST

Chickens
Sabatier sacrificial knife
His'n'hers toilet buckets
Coffee maker (female)
Bagel maker (either sex)
~~Concubine~~
Harry Potter menorah
Roman citizenship
Wine rack

THY-FACE.COM

Jesus Christ

✉ Jesus Christ attended the event Marriage at Cana. • Saith • Liketh

 John Zebedee Jesus! My mouth feels like a camel's armpit! What a wedding! What was in that wine?
🕓 Wednesday 7 June 30AD at 4:04pm • Saith • Liketh

 James Zebedee They only had water when I got there. I thought uh-oh, Seventh Day Adventist alert! But thank God for the Virgin Mary! She stood in the middle of the dancefloor with an empty glass screaming, "I want more wine! Fetch me more wine!" Everyone was like, there isn't any more wine. Then Jesus waved his hand over these urns of water and turned the water into wine. It was like totally the coolest thing I've ever seen.
🕓 Wednesday 7 June 30AD at 4:09pm

 Virgin Mary did i tell you i once met arkAngel gabriel?
🕓 Wednesday 7 June 30AD at 4:10pm • Saith • Liketh

 John Zebedee lol! All the time, Auntie Mary. Maybe you should go and have a lie down now :*) hic!
🕓 Wednesday 7 June 30AD at 4:15pm

 John Mark You were totally mental, JZ! Coming dressed as a leper! When your hand dropped off during the ceremony, I thought the bride's mum was gonna freak!
🕓 Wednesday 7 June 30AD at 5:18pm

 Jesus Christ It's all very funny ha-ha for you guys, but I'm being prosecuted by the Galilean Wine and Spirits Authority for producing wine without a licence. Does anyone know a good lawyer?
🕓 Wednesday 7 June 30AD at 5:57pm. • Saith • Liketh

❗ Jesus Christ and Reuben the Lawyer are now friends. • Saith • Liketh
388 similar stories

View Mine Icons (11)

Edit Mine Profile

Miracle Worker

Personal Information

Birthday	Dwelleth
25 December	**Cana**

Website:
www.bornagaininme.il

Proclamations

THYFACE **maps**

The Known World, as seen from Heaven. Find your own cave!

👍 Liketh 👎 Despiseth

Male, aged 30?

Top quality footwear for the busy exec! Be smart *and* fashionable!

👍 Liketh 👎 Despiseth

Loggeth out

Friends
Jesus Christ hath 21183 friends
See all
Find more friends

 Judas Iscariot   John Mark   Simon Zelotes   James Zebedee

Inland Revenue Service
of the Emperor and People of
Rome (but mainly the Emperor)

SPQR

Your name

Matthew Levi

Your address

Crown & Anchor, Capernaum

EXPENSES CLAIM FORM

ITEM	AMOUNT
Donkey mileage – 135 miles @ 5 shekels per mile	675sh
Subsistence – 38 days @ 12 shekels a day	456sh
4 stone tablets + chisel & mallet	86sh
Accommodation – 5 nights in 3-star stable	440sh
Pair of safety sandals	23sh
Web hosting	132sh
Daily scrolls	212sh
Foot washing oil	512sh
Second cave allowance	62tal
Adult scroll rental	56sh
Candle & heating	101sh
Charity donation	1sh

Jesus Christ

HATH COME TO PASS

💬 Jesus Christ formed the group Apostles of Jesus. • Saith • Liketh

🐟 Andrew the Fish joined the group Apostles of Jesus. • Saith • Liketh

🐟 Simon Peter joined the group Apostles of Jesus. • Saith • Liketh

10 similar stories

View Mine Icons (11)

Edit Mine Profile

Lord of the Apostles

 Matthew Levi Great to be on board, Jesus! As you know, I used to work for the Inland Revenue Service, and you'd be amazed how much you can write off in this game if you know the ropes.
🕐 Friday 23 June 30AD at 1:15pm • Saith • Liketh

Personal Information

Status	Dwelleth
Single	**Galilee**

Website:
www.bornagaininme.il

> John Zebedee I once wrote off a camel! Totalled it on the road to Ninevah trying to overtake a caravan.
> 🕐 Friday 23 June 30AD at 1:17pm

Proclamations

Webuyanycamel.com

> Matthew Levi That's not what I meant. For a start, if you're preaching more than 13 miles from home, you can claim 12 shekels a day subsistence, even if you're fasting. You don't even have to provide a receipt!.
> 🕐 Friday 23 June 30AD at 1:20pm

Just ask for Mick the Butcher.

👍 Liketh 🗨 Despiseth

> Doubting Thomas I seriously doubt that.
> 🕐 Friday 23 June 30AD at 1:31pm

Wonders of the Modern World

> Andrew the Fish Don't forget, I can get fish at cost.
> 🕐 Friday 23 June 30AD at 1:44pm

> Simon Peter Big deal! We can all get fish at cost!
> 🕐 Friday 23 June 30AD at 1:50pm

Visit the Great Pyramid and the other Wonders of the Modern World on our luxury cruise.

> Simon Zelotes So when do we start mashing heads?
> 🕐 Friday 23 June 30AD at 1:51pm

👍 Liketh 🗨 Despiseth

 Jesus Christ Guys, guys, I'm not entirely sure you understand what we're going to be doing here.
🕐 Friday 23 June 30AD at 2:11pm • Saith • Liketh

 Simon Peter I know! I know! We're going to be teaching people that God is great, sins can be forgiven and Matthew is a loser.
🕐 Friday 23 June 30AD at 2:13pm • Saith • Liketh

 Jesus Christ Well, two out of three. See, Peter might look like an Easter Island statue, but at least he's getting with the programme!
🕐 Friday 23 June 30AD at 2:18pm • Saith • Liketh

Loggeth out

Friends
Jesus Christ hath 23458 friends
See all
Find more friends

 Matthew Levi

 Doubting Thomas

 Apostle Philip

 Nicodemus ben Gurion

THY-FACE.COM

Simon the Pharisee

❗ Simon the Leper changed his name to Simon the Pharisee. • Saith • Liketh

 Jesus Christ Thanks again for inviting me round for supper last night, Simon. I hope you liked the wine?
⏱ Friday 23 September 30AD at 2:12pm • Saith • Liketh

 Simon the Pharisee 100 shekels and I don't post this icon of you on ThouTube! Only kiddin'! But what in the known world were you doing letting that Mary Magdalene woman slaver all over your feet all through supper? You know, I could swear I've met her before.
⏱ Friday 23 September 30AD at 2:36pm • Saith • Liketh

 John Zebedee What? Was Maggers there? From the anointing parlour on Sodom Street? If I'd realised it was gonna be that kind of party, I might have tipped up!
⏱ Friday 23 September 30AD at 2:44pm

 Simon the Pharisee My mistake. Now I come to think about it, she wasn't at all familiar. Don't take this the wrong way, Jesus, but IMHO you're hanging out with the wrong crowd if you want to make a go of this preaching lark. My Pharisee buddies love all this Messianic guff, but they're dreadful snobs when it comes to fallen women.
⏱ Friday 23 September 30AD at 2:45pm • Saith • Liketh

 Jesus Christ Come on, Simon, I'm here to save sinners. I can hardly do that by correspondence, can I?
⏱ Friday 23 September 30AD at 2:48pm. • Saith • Liketh

 John Zebedee Exactly. We don't hang out with harlots for fun, you know ;-)
⏱ Friday 23 September 30AD at 2:49pm

View Mine Icons (4)
Edit Mine Profile

Law-abiding Pharisee

Personal Information

Dwelleth
Bethany

Son of
**Gamaliel ben Simeon
Chief Pharisee**

Website:
www.votepharisee.gal

Proclamations

The No 1 Pharisee scroll

Loggeth out

Friends
Simon the Pharisee hath 127 friends
See all
Find more friends

 Tim the Pharisee
 Gamaliel b Simeon
 Mrs Simon Pharisee
 Nicodemus ben Gurion

Fornication and the City

IN AMPHITHEATRES SEPTEMBER 20TH

Mary Magdalene

HATH COME TO PASS

 Mary Magdalene's favourite show is Fornication and the City. • Saith • Liketh

 Mary Magdalene hath changed her status to Available. • Saith • Liketh

 John Zebedee Hey Maggers, I hear you got off with my main man Jesus Christ last night!
🕐 Friday 23 September 30AD at 2:51pm • Saith • Liketh

 Mary Magdalene No way! Who told you that? We were chatting that's all. Do you know him then?
🕐 Friday 23 September 30AD at 2:52pm

 John Zebedee Not in the Biblical sense! lol! Jesus is my cousin, dude. I'm his right-hand man!
🕐 Friday 23 September 30AD at 2:54pm

 Joanna Chuza He won't need a "right-hand man" if Mary gets her mitts on him!
🕐 Friday 23 September 30AD at 3:05pm

 James Zebedee ☌ Liketh this!
🕐 Friday 23 September 30AD at 3:06pm

 Martha Magdalene Are we talking about THE Jesus Christ? The wine merchant?
🕐 Friday 23 September 30AD at 3:40pm • Saith • Liketh

 Mary Magdalene He's not a wine merchant! He's a doctor!
🕐 Friday 23 September 30AD at 3:43pm

 Lazarus Magdalene Oh Mary! You met a doctor and you didn't bring him round to see me? You know I'm ill.
🕐 Friday 23 September 30AD at 3:43pm

 Mary Magdalene Sorry. I forgot to mention my brother had man-flu :-o
🕐 Friday 23 September 30AD at 3:45pm

 John Zebedee Jesus isn't a doctor, dude, he's a Messiah!
🕐 Friday 23 September 30AD at 3:46pm

Mary Magdalene That's what you say! But he healed me! He said I had seven unclean spirits in me!
🕐 Friday 23 September 30AD at 3:49pm

Joanna Chuza I remember that night! lol!
🕐 Friday 23 September 30AD at 3:53pm

View Mine Icons (453)

Edit Mine Profile

Jesus loves me!

Personal Information

Birthday	Status
22 July	**Available**

Website:
www.anointmebad.com

Proclamations

Give in to temptation!

You won't "Adam and Eve" our range of sexy underwear.

☌ Liketh 🖐 Despiseth

Want a new hair colour?

Stylish hair for powerless women.
Because you're worthless.

☌ Liketh 🖐 Despiseth

Loggeth out

Friends
Mary Magdalene hath 11643 friends
See all
Find more friends

 Martha Magdalene
 Joanna Chuza
 Lazarus Magdalene
 Susanna Myrbarer

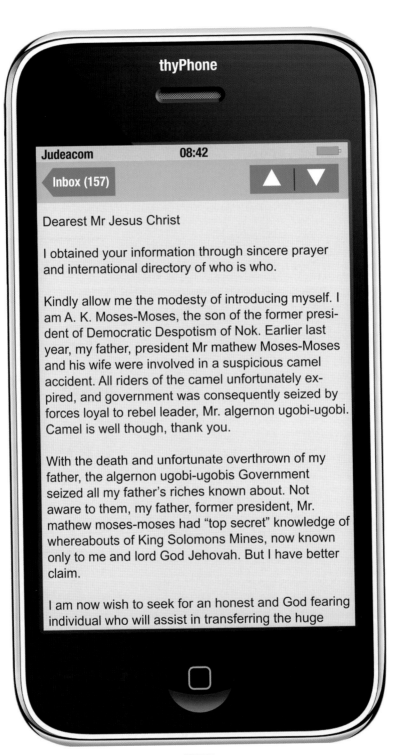

thyPhone

Dearest Mr Jesus Christ

I obtained your information through sincere prayer and international directory of who is who.

Kindly allow me the modesty of introducing myself. I am A. K. Moses-Moses, the son of the former president of Democratic Despotism of Nok. Earlier last year, my father, president Mr mathew Moses-Moses and his wife were involved in a suspicious camel accident. All riders of the camel unfortunately expired, and government was consequently seized by forces loyal to rebel leader, Mr. algernon ugobi-ugobi. Camel is well though, thank you.

With the death and unfortunate overthrown of my father, the algernon ugobi-ugobis Government seized all my father's riches known about. Not aware to them, my father, former president, Mr. mathew moses-moses had "top secret" knowledge of whereabouts of King Solomons Mines, now known only to me and lord God Jehovah. But I have better claim.

I am now wish to seek for an honest and God fearing individual who will assist in transferring the huge

THY-FACE.COM

Jesus Christ

 John Zebedee Respect, dude! Great way to celebrate Passover, trashing the offices of the Temple Moneychangers!
🕐 Wednesday 21 March 31AD at 6:11pm • Saith • Liketh

 Jesus Christ I know I'm normally meek and mild, but I was really flipping angry. Did you seen the scrolls yesterday? We're heading for global economic meltdown, unemployment is off the scale, yet the Temple Moneychangers have been paying themselves millions of talents in bonuses!
🕐 Wednesday 21 March 31AD at 6:15pm

 Doubting Thomas Don't believe everything you read in the scrolls.
🕐 Wednesday 21 March 31AD at 6:17pm

 James Zebedee Your mum was the best. Standing at the bottom of Moneychangers Tower shouting "Jump you bast*rds!"
🕐 Wednesday 21 March 31AD at 6:25pm.

 John Zebedee Seriously, your mum is such a MILF.
🕐 Wednesday 21 March 31AD at 6:30pm

 Virgin Mary I'm such a what? What's a MILF?
🕐 Wednesday 21 March 31AD at 6:32pm

 Jesus Christ 🔨 would like to smite John Zebedee. Don't worry, mum. It means "Mums In Lovely Frocks", doesn't it guys?
🕐 Wednesday 21 March 31AD at 6:33pm

 Judas Iscariot Are you sure it means "frocks"?
🕐 Wednesday 21 March 31AD at 6:34pm

 James Zebedee Frocking sure!
🕐 Wednesday 21 March 31AD at 6:37pm.

John Zebedee lol
🕐 Wednesday 21 March 31AD at 6:39pm

View Mine Icons (12)

Edit Mine Profile

Anti-Globalisation Protester

Personal Information

Status | Dwelleth
Single | **Jerusalem**

Website:
www.bornagaininme.il

Proclamations

Pimp Thy Ride

You can be cool in the desert!

🖒 Liketh 🖓 Despiseth

Everything must go!

It's a steal (except we won't cut your hand off!)

🖒 Liketh 🖓 Despiseth

Loggeth out

Friends
Jesus Christ hath 31025 friends
See all
Find more friends

 Mary Magdalene   John Zebedee   Judas Iscariot   James the Less

Sermon on the Mount (first draft)

~~Today is not a day for soundbites. We can leave those at home. But I feel the hand of history upon me.~~

~~Friends, Jews, countrymen.~~

~~Two Pharisees walk into a bar~~

~~Blessed are the poor, for they shall get a pay rise, win the lottery, they shall be rich, for ye shall be given two ha'pennies~~ for theirs is the kingdom of God (yes!) ~~Blessed are the ugly, for they shall benefit from the invention of beer (encore gag??)~~

Blessed are those that hunger, ~~for they shall have dinner (bit weak)~~ for they shall be filled (good!).

Blessed are ye that weep, for ye shall laugh out loud. Blessed are ye when people misunderstand you, ~~and try to use your healing powers to make themselves rich, and send you nasty legal letters when you're only trying to help people and all they ever really want you to do is perform miracles~~

Jesus Christ

 Apostle Philip Took these great icons of the Sermon on the Mount. Wicked gig, by the way. People will be talking about it for weeks!

⏲ Friday 23 March 31AD at 2:30pm • Saith • Liketh

 James Zebedee Loved the gag about the two blind dudes who fell in a ditch! Well funny.
⏲ Friday 23 March 31AD at 2:45pm

 John Zebedee Yeah, didn't see that coming! lol!
⏲ Friday 23 March 31AD at 2:49pm

 Matthew Levi Me and the boys from the Revenue had a right laugh over that stuff about "false profits"!
⏲ Friday 23 March 31AD at 3:13pm

 Andrew the Fish When you said "Blessed are ye that hunger now, for ye shall be filled", it really struck a chord with those of us whose tummies were rumbling. I know I keep going on about it, but next time we must have professional catering.
⏲ Friday 23 March 31AD at 4:52pm

 Simon Peter I liked the bit when you said, "Blessed are ye, when men shall hate you." I didn't think you were gonna mention Matthew directly!!
⏲ Friday 23 March 31AD at 6:15pm

 Simon Zelotes Excellent idea telling people to turn the other cheek when you deck 'em. Lets you smite the living daylights out of them!
⏲ Friday 23 March 31AD at 8:18pm

 Jesus Christ Thanks guys. That's great. You really got it.
⏲ Friday 23 March 31AD at 8:20pm.

HATH COME TO PASS

 Jesus Christ hath healed Roman Centurion's servant.

🕊 15678 people despiseth this. • Saith • Liketh

View Mine Icons (14)

Edit Mine Profile

> Part-time lecturer

Personal Information

Birthday	Status
25 December	**Single**

Website:
www.bornagaininme.il

Proclamations

Crippled by debt?

Why not sell yourself into slavery? Visit Happy Slaves™ for a free quotation. All colours accepted.

👍 Liketh 🗨 Despiseth

Cash-4-Concubines

We buy your old or unwanted concubines for cash. ACT NOW!

👍 Liketh 🗨 Despiseth

Loggeth out

Friends
Jesus Christ hath 41252 friends
See all
Find more friends

 Virgin Mary

 John the Baptist

Simon Zelotes

Andrew the Fish

My top tipple of the year

Regular correspondent and wine aficionado Virgin Mary chooses her favourite wine of the past 12 months.

L ast year I attended a marriage in Cana, and boy, am I glad I did! They served the most glorious full-bodied red wine I've tasted in years.

Although extremely young, this bright ruby-red wine opens with a fruity black cherry-like bouquet with gushes of strawberry and hints of menthol and cinnamon.

Despite significant tannic structure, the palate is already showing generous, concentrated flavours of perfectly ripened black and red fruits interlaced with graphite, baked bread and chocolate sorbet. The finish is dry, and its nicely managed tannins linger on the tongue like a gift from Jehovah.

Particularly good with goat.

THY-FACE.COM

Virgin Mary

 Jesus Christ Hi mum! Sorry I haven't been home for a while. The apostles and I have been "spreading the word" in Samaria. Met a lovely woman by Jacob's Well, and had a fab chat (have posted a couple of icons below). Then she brought all the people out of the city and I told them all about God and we sang some songs and had a really groovy time. I'd definitely go again, but it would be good to come home for a bit, do some preaching in Nazareth.

⏱ Monday 9 July 31AD at 6:23pm • Saith • Liketh

 James Zebedee I can't help thinking he missed a trick with the well, Auntie Mary. Lots of water and not enough "waving of the hand", if you get my drift!
⏱ Monday 9 July 31AD at 6:25pm

 Kevin of Nazareth Is that your Jesus? Joseph's son?
⏱ Monday 9 July 31AD at 6:26pm • Saith • Liketh

 John Zebedee There are two schools of thought. Did you ever see My Two Dads?
⏱ Monday 9 July 31AD at 6:27pm

Jesus Christ Ignore him, he art an idiot. I am yes.
⏱ Monday 9 July 31AD at 6:31pm

Kevin of Nazareth No disrespect to you, Mary, but your Jesus isn't welcome in Nazareth. He's spent the past 12 months doing his magic tricks for those Samaritans, and he hasn't rustled up so much as a bottle of Blue Nun for his own people.
⏱ Monday 9 July 31AD at 6:34pm

 Virgin Mary Don't you take any notice, sweetie. We'd all love to see you. And you should go and see John the Baptist too. Visiting days are first Thursday of the month. By the way, I've been giving some thought to your next miracle. Have you ever tried gin?
⏱ Monday 9 July 31AD at 6:39pm

View Mine Icons (20)

Edit Mine Profile

> Mother of God

Personal Information

Birthday
8 September

Status
Not even looking!

Website:
www.virginmothers.com

Loggeth out

Friends
Virgin Mary hath 174 friends
See all
Find more friends

Kevin of Nazareth | Joseph of Arimathea | Jack of Daniels | Robin of Loxley

BEELZEBUB, WORMWOOD & ASSOCIATES

Jesus Christ esq
By hand

31 July 31 AD

Dear Mr Christ

My firm has recently been retained by Lord Satan, Prince of Darkness, following your unprovoked eviction on Thursday last of one of his devils from a man in Galilee. I must insist you cease and desist any activity relating to the exorcism, eviction or casting out of unclean spirits, devils or sundry demons. Failure to do so could result in a lengthy and costly civil action being brought against you by my client.

Yours, &c

Mephistopheles

Senior Partner

THY-FACE.COM

Jesus Christ

Jesus Christ took the ThyFace test Which God Are You Most Like?

Jesus Christ is most like Vulcan, God of Carpenters • Saith • Liketh

 James Zebedee That accounts for the pointy ears then!
⏱ Wednesday 1 August 31AD at 9:12pm

View Mine Icons (11)

Edit Mine Profile

Pro bono medical worker

 Jesus Christ Flipping heck! They moan when I heal on the Sabbath and turn water into wine. Now they're moaning because I cast out devils. Blessed are the moaners! Hey, that gives me an idea for another sermon.
⏱ Thursday 2 August 31AD at 8:35am • Saith • Liketh

Personal Information

Birthday
25 December

Status
Single

Website:
www.bornagaininme.il

 Judas Iscariot Maybe I should scrub "casting out of devils" from the price list. What do you think?
⏱ Thursday 2 August 31AD at 11:42am

 Jesus Christ What price list? What are you talking about?
⏱ Thursday 2 August 31AD at 11:43am

Proclamations

Discount Scroll Club

 Judas Iscariot Johnny Zee said you'd OK'd it.
⏱ Thursday 2 August 31AD at 11:52am

 John Zebedee Yeah, I meant to tell you. Thing is, ever since your second miracle of curing the little boy in Capernaum, which was great by the way, we've been inundated with requests for you to heal people.
⏱ Thursday 2 August 31AD at 11:55am

Buy the first Dead Sea Scroll and get the second half price! Plus: free monkey in a fez!

👍 Liketh 👎 Despiseth

 Jesus Christ But I have been healing people.
⏱ Thursday 2 August 31AD at 11:57am

Unemployed? No friends?

 John Zebedee I know you have. But as most of them don't have insurance, we're having to charge for treatment. We're not Communists, are we? Ten shekels for a headache, 50 for a withered arm, and a talent for full-blown leprosy. We weren't sure what to charge for casting out of devils anyway – some of them are clearly faking to get attention. We'll just scrub it from the list.
⏱ Thursday 2 August 31AD at 12:01pm

 Jesus Christ You'll scrub the whole list! If my ministry was about making money, I'd be preaching in Utah, not this dump.
⏱ Thursday 2 August 31AD at 12:03pm

👍 Liketh 👎 Despiseth

 John Zebedee Well forgive me! I doth repent! Blah-de-blah-de-blah. Who ever heard of a religion that wasn't out to make money?
⏱ Thursday 2 August 31AD at 12:06pm

Loggeth out

Friends)
Jesus Christ hath 43425 friends
See all
Find more friends

 Martha Magdalene

 John Mark

James the Less

Apostle Philip

XXXV

That's Why Herodias Art A Tramp
(words by Baptist, music by Rogers/Baptist)

🖩≶[Download tinny ringtone for 10 shekels]

She fornicates – with princes and earls
Struts like a harlot – in diamonds and pearls
She whores like Satan's – Bab'lonian girls
That's why Herodias art a tramp

She art damnéd – and lightning will strike
She ruts with uncles – and brothers alike
That's why she's known – as the Judean bike
That's why Heriodias art a tramp

She loves to whore – more – I can't begin
Life full of sin
A bawd
Oh Lord!
Tupped by each soldier – in Pontius's camp
That's why Heriodias art a tramp

She art the strumpet – that trumpets my fate
She'd like to serve up – my head on a plate
She won't be happy – until I am late
That's why Heriodias art a tramp

🖩≶[Download tinny ringtone for 10 shekels]

THY-FACE.COM

Jesus Christ

 Virgin Mary Hi poppet. It's months since you've been in touch! Why not come home for your birthday (and bring a bottle of your mum's favourite vino)?
⏱ Monday 20 September 31AD at 1:30pm • Saith • Liketh

 Jesus Christ They tried to throw me off a cliff last time I came home! That said, I do fancy a bit of me-time. After my last sermon I booked a cheap cruise on the Sea of Galilee. But when I turned up, who should be waiting for me but 12 apostles and a multitude of disciples? Blessed art I! The sea was very choppy and there was much wailing and gnashing of teeth!
⏱ Monday 20 September 31AD at 5:50pm

 Apostle Philip Still a bit puzzled by your last parable, Jesus. What was the stony ground again? Was it Satan?
⏱ Monday 20 September 31AD at 6:21pm • Saith • Liketh

 Simon Peter Was it Satan? lol! The fowl of the air were Satan, you great buffoon. Everyone got that. The stony ground represents material riches.
⏱ Monday 20 September 31AD at 6:28pm

 Jude Thaddeus What a load of bollocks! The thorns were material riches.
⏱ Monday 20 September 31AD at 6:30pm

 James the Less So what was the stony ground then? Was it the word of God?
⏱ Monday 20 September 31AD at 6:32pm

 Apostle Philip How can the stony ground be the word of God? The scattered seeds are the word of God. That's the whole point of the story.
⏱ Monday 20 September 31AD at 6:37pm

 James the Less Well, some seeds look like stones.
⏱ Monday 20 September 31AD at 6:41pm

Simon Peter What can that even mean?
⏱ Monday 20 September 31AD at 6:42pm

 Jesus Christ You know what, guys, I think you're ready to go and preach on your own now – in twos, like we discussed. I'm sure you'll all do really well.
⏱ Monday 20 September 31AD at 6:55pm

Doubting Thomas I'll believe that when I see it.
⏱Monday 20 September 31AD at 6:56pm

View Mine Icons (15)
Edit Mine Profile

Teacher of men

Personal Information

Birthday
25 December

Dwelleth
Galilee

Website:
www.bornagaininme.il

Proclamations

Machaerus Prison Blues

 The stunning new album from John the Baptist written and recorded from his prison cell. Featuring "Behold the Lamb of God" and "That's Why Herodias Art A Tramp".

👍 Liketh 👎 Despiseth

Last minute caravan holidays

All the fun of the open desert with none of the tiresome luxuries you get with other holidays!

👍 Liketh 👎 Despiseth

Loggeth out

Friends
Jesus Christ hath 44785 friends
See all
Find more friends

 Virgin Mary
 Jude Thaddeus
 Simon Peter
 Herod Philip

The ☗ Mail

ON SABBATH

Herod Antipas vows to stand shoulder-to-shoulder with Tiberius as the Emperor talks of 'special relationship'.

HEROD SUPPORTS WAR ON TERROR

Herod Antipas has confirmed his commitment to Rome's War on Terror in a speech delivered on the eve of his fifty-third birthday.

The tetrarch, who has come under fire from the loony liberal left for his indefinite detainment of the radical cleric John the Baptist, said, "the people who moan about detention without trial are themselves friends of the terrorists. Rome has always enjoyed a special relationship with the Jew-

EXCLUSIVE
by **Josephus ben Matthias**
Royal Correspondent

ish people, and I am grateful for this opportunity to demonstrate my support for the Emperor."

Judean governor Pontius Pilate added, "The universal appeal of totalitarianism will ultimately triumph over radical notions of freedom and democracy, just as it brought down the Walls of Jericho."

Herod Antipas: "standing shoulder-to-shoulder with the Emperor."

INSIDE: Herod Salome on life after Big Brethren
See pages 7, 8 and 9

Herod Antipas

Herod Antipas Oh God! I got so drunk last night. My head feels like Goliath's after three rounds with David. I can't remember a thing about the party!
⏱ Saturday 15 March 32AD at 4:18pm • Saith • Liketh

Herod Agrippa Uncle, do you think I could get that 1000 talents you promised me last night?
⏱ Saturday 15 March 32AD at 4:20pm

Herod Antipas I promised you 1000 talents?
⏱ Saturday 15 March 32AD at 4:22pm

Chuza the Steward That's nothing compared to what you gave Salome! My Joanna nearly split her sides!
⏱ Saturday 15 March 32AD at 4:24pm

Herod Antipas Oh lord! What did my stepdaughter con out of me this time? I didn't promise to get her on Celebrity Dancing on Sand, did I?
⏱ Saturday 15 March 32AD at 4:26pm

Herod Agrippa No, you said if she did the veil dance you'd give her anything, up to half your kingdom.
⏱Saturday 15 March 32AD at 4:28pm

Herod Antipas I didn't give it her, did I? I couldn't survive that, not on top of all these riots we've been having since I banged up John the Baptist.
⏱ Saturday 15 March 32AD at 4:30pm

Chuza the Steward Funnily enough, it involved the Baptist. Honestly, you wouldn't recognise him now.
⏱ Saturday 15 March 32AD at 4:33pm

Herod Antipas Has he lost a bit of weight?
⏱ Saturday 15 March 32AD at 4:36pm

Herodias And a bit of height! lol! Remember this?
⏱ Saturday 15 March 32AD at 4:39pm

Herod Antipas Shit.
⏱ Saturday 15 March 32AD at 4:45pm.

View Mine Icons (22)

Edit Mine Profile

> **Ruler of Galilee and Perea**

Personal Information

Status
Living in sin (and loving it!)

Website:
www.ethnarchofgalilee.gov.gal

Proclamations

Ascension Stairlifts

Over 50? Mobility problems? Our practical solutions include chair and detachable slaves.

👍 Liketh 👎 Despiseth

No longer a babe magnet?

Try Grecian 1000 – the natural way to keep those youthful looks!

👍 Liketh 👎 Despiseth

Loggeth out

Friends
Herod Antipas hath 653 friends
See all
Find more friends

Herod Salome   Tiberius Caesar   Joanna Chuza   Herodias

John the Baptist Action Figure

Now with detachable head!

Pull cord in back for ten phrases, including:

"Behold! The Lamb of God!"

"Repent ye! For the Kingdom of Heaven is at hand"

"Herodias shall burn in the fiery pits of Hell for all eternity!"

"Please don't chop off my head!"

Jesus Christ

HATH COME TO PASS

 John the Baptist's status hath been changed to Decapitated.

 John Zebedee Hey Jesus! We're back man, we been a-preachin' and a-teachin' that good word, good word, that good ole word o' the Lord! What a bummer about John the Baptist, though! Hey, maybe you could raise him from the dead like you did that kid in Nain? I'll bring the head, James'll get the body and Maggers can bring her sewing kit!
🕐 Sunday 16 March 32AD at 3.50pm • Saith • Liketh

> Mary Magdalene You are such a sicko, Zebbers! There's nothing we can do, I suppose?
> 🕐 Sunday 16 March 32AD at 3.52pm

> James Zebedee I'm not a medical man, but I've reviewed the literature, and frankly it's not promising.
> 🕐 Sunday 16 March 32AD at 3.55pm

 Jesus Christ Have you been away six months already? How did the preaching tour go? All get on OK?
🕐 Sunday 16 March 32AD at 8.44pm • Saith • Liketh

> Simon Peter Great! Andrew and I cast out devils!
> 🕐 Sunday 16 March 32AD at 8.49pm

> Apostle Philip And I cured a leper in Jaffa while John Mark went off to minister to some sailors he met.
> 🕐 Sunday 16 March 32AD at 9.12pm

> Matthew Levi I tried faith healing, and might've done OK if you hadn't saddled me with Thomas.
> 🕐 Sunday 16 March 32AD at 9.31pm

> James the Less Thaddeus and I found some lost sheep like you told us. Shepherds were very happy.
> 🕐 Sunday 16 March 32AD at 9.57pm

> Simon Zelotes Judas and I didn't kill anyone. Honest.
> 🕐 Sunday 16 March 32AD at 9.59pm.

> John Zebedee And James and I released a celebrity single for the Gaza earthquake. Went straight to number one. How rock'n'roll is that!?
> 🕐 Sunday 16 March 32AD at 11.05pm

 Jesus Christ What can I say? Once again you all completely surpassed my expectations.
🕐 Sunday 16 March 32AD at 11.19pm • Saith • Liketh

View Mine Icons (24)

Edit Mine Profile

Just Jesus

Personal Information

Birthday	Status
25 December	**Single**

Website:
www.bornagaininme.il

Proclamations

Keep warm with a real fire

Camel dung: the original, the best.

👍 Liketh 👎 Despiseth

Commemorate the Baptist

Celebrate the life of John the Baptist with this tasteful, hand-painted china plate.

👍 Liketh 👎 Despiseth

Loggeth out

Friends)
Jesus Christ hath 47125 friends
See all
Find more friends

 Simon the Pharisee   Jude Thaddeus   Apostle Philip   Joseph of Arimathea

THY-FACE.COM

Andrew the Fish

 Andrew the Fish joined the group Friends of the Pilchard. • Saith • Liketh
116 similar stories

 Andrew the Fish I'm so excited! In two days time, Jesus is playing his biggest gig yet – in front of 5000 people – and I've been put in charge of catering!
🕐 Wednesday 19 March 32AD at 2:16pm • Saith • Liketh

> Simon Peter So what we having, bro? No, don't tell me. Fish.
> 🕐 Wednesday 19 March 32AD at 2:44pm

> Andrew the Fish Yes, but not just any fish. I'm thinking Jerk-spiced red snapper. With rice and peas and crusty bread. Get a bit of a Caribbean theme going.
> 🕐 Wednesday 19 March 32AD at 2:48pm

 Jesus Christ Hi Andrew. I've been reviewing the catering arrangements, and I think we're being a bit ambitious. I reckon we can get by with five loaves and, say, two fishes.
🕐 Wednesday 19 March 32AD at 4:33pm • Saith • Liketh

> Andrew the Fish WTF! I presume we're talking about the Loch Ness Monster and the fish that swallowed Jonah?
> 🕐 Wednesday 19 March 32AD at 4:35pm

> Jesus Christ Ye of little faith. Seriously, two fish, five loaves and no foreign muck. Gives me the runs.
> 🕐 Wednesday 19 March 32AD at 4:37pm

> James the Less Should we bring a bottle?
> 🕐 Wednesday 19 March 32AD at 4:41pm

> Andrew the Fish A half bottle should do it!
> 🕐 Wednesday 19 March 32AD at 4:44pm

> James the Less Right you are then!
> 🕐 Wednesday 19 March 32AD at 4:47pm

 Josh the Baker Hey Andrew. Just read the posting from your boss. He's joking, right? I've bought a new camel off the back of this order.
🕐 Thursday 20 March 32AD at 7:02am • Saith • Liketh

🔄 Andrew the Fish changed his status to Missing. • Saith • Liketh

---

View Mine Icons (4)

Edit Mine Profile

First Apostle of Jesus

Personal Information

Birthday	Status
30 November	**Separated**

Website:
www.incodwetrust.net

Loggeth out

Friends
Andrew the Fish hath 62 friends
See all
Find more friends

 Simon Peter
 Mick the Butcher
 Josh the Baker
 Candlestick Maker

John Zebedee

 John Zebedee I've just seen THE funniest thing in the world! We were all like in this boat, and Jesus. OMG! We were in this boat, and who came walking across the water towards us, but Jesus? And I mean walking ON THE WATER. But that's not the funny bit. I am crying here. Simon Peter looks out at Jesus and says, "hey if Jesus can walk on water, so can I!" Then he jumps in the water and sinks like a brick! LMFAO! What a total retard! Jesus had to reach in and pull him out again!

◷ Saturday 22 March 32AD at 11:03pm • Saith • Liketh

 James Zebedee He truly is a fisher of men! lol!
◷ Saturday 22 March 32AD at 11:10pm

 Jesus Christ Sorry you can't make it tomorrow, John. Apparently, the Mount's been booked by some stupid boy band, so we're having to make do with the Hill. According to Health & Safety, it only holds 4000.

◷ Sunday 31 August 32AD at 9:30am • Saith • Liketh

 Andrew the Fish 4000? Should I bring a cheese sandwich?
◷ Sunday 31 August 32AD at 9:41am

 Jesus Christ Oh Andrew, I wish you'd let it go.
◷ Sunday 31 August 32AD at 9:43am

 Matthew Levi My maths skills might prove useful here. If you had five loaves and two fishes for 5000, then you need four loaves and 1.6 fishes for 4000.
◷ Sunday 31 August 32AD at 9:52pm

 Andrew the Fish Right, I'll just pop and get 1.6 fishes then, shall I? You great pillock.
◷ Sunday 31 August 32AD at 9:56pm

View Mine Icons (15312)

Edit Mine Profile

Apostle and Rock Star

Personal Information

Birthday	Status
27 December	**Come and get me**

Website:
www.planetzebedee.com

Proclamations

Loggeth out

Friends
John Zebedee hath 48213 friends
See all
Find more friends

 Virgin Mary

 Herod Salome

Mary Magdalene

Whore of Babylon

PHARISEE GUIDE TO HEALTH & CLEANLINESS

WARNING:
WASH YOUR HANDS THEN BURN AFTER READING. THEN WASH YOUR HANDS AGAIN, SAY A PRAYER AND CROSS YOUR FINGERS. WASH YOUR FINGERS, WASH YOUR HANDS AGAIN AND SAY ANOTHER PRAYER JUST TO BE ON THE SAFE SIDE

VOLUME CLXVII

THY-FACE.COM

Jesus Christ

🔊 Jesus Christ hath healed a deaf man.

🔊 I SAID, JESUS CHRIST HATH HEALED A DEAF MAN.

View Mine Icons (26)

Edit Mine Profile

Man With A Mission

 Simon the Pharisee My fellow Pharisees are on the warpath again. They came to your last gig and noticed some of your disciples eating bread without washing their hands. You know that not washing your hands before a meal is the 2,365,427th abomination mentioned in the scriptures. The one just before the snowman.
⏰ Tuesday 2 September 32AD at 1:31pm • Saith • Liketh

Personal Information

Birthday	Status
25 December	**It's complicated**

Website:
www.bornagaininme.il

> Virgin Mary I can guess who he's talking about, John Zebedee! You were always a mucky little pixie. Not like John the Baptist. He was never out of the river.
> ⏰ Tuesday 2 September 32AD at 1:43pm

> John Zebedee Oh Auntie Mary, John the Baptist smelt like a camel's loincloth, and you know it.
> ⏰ Tuesday 2 September 32AD at 4:44pm

Proclamations

Possessed by Demons?

Let our exorcists cast them out*

 Nicodemus ben Gurion Simon's right. They've reported you to the High Priest, Joseph ben Caiaphas, and he's a total prig!
⏰ Tuesday 2 September 32AD at 5:20pm • Saith • Liketh

> Jesus Christ You tell Caiaphas it's not what goes into a man's mouth that defiles him, but what comes out of it.
> ⏰ Tuesday 2 September 32AD at 5:31pm

* remember, if you fail to make regular payments, your soul may be repossessed.

👍 Liketh 👎 Despiseth

> John Zebedee That's what John Mark always says!
> ⏰ Tuesday 2 September 32AD at 5:31pm

> James Zebedee lol!
> ⏰ Tuesday 2 September 32AD at 5:31pm

> John Mark Honestly! You boys are so naughty!
> ⏰ Tuesday 2 September 32AD at 5:32pm

Everyone likes a smart ass!

 Simon the Pharisee Anyway, I've sent you a copy of the Pharisee Guide to Health & Cleanliness. Please get your clowns to read it.
⏰ Tuesday 2 September 32AD at 5:49pm • Saith • Liketh

Redefining urban riding and parking. Test-ride one today.

👍 Liketh 👎 Despiseth

> Simon Zelotes Oi! You're not too big for a good smiting!
> ⏰ Tuesday 2 September 32AD at 5:51pm.

Loggeth out

Friends
Jesus Christ hath 49651 friends
See all
Find more friends

 Geoff the Leper

 Ol' Ma Zebedee

 Merope Pleiad

Queen Boudicca

IS MAGGERS PREGGERS?

THE JUDEAN Enquirer

WORLD EXCLUSIVE NEWS

Reconstruction

Only in The ENQUIRER

Brutus the Gladiator texts NAKED icons to mistress

ALIENS ABDUCT MAN IN WHITE!

Eye-witnesses see 'shining figure' floating in sky

CELEBRITY NOSE JOBS
whose are REAL whose are FAKE

Herod Salome

Claudia Procula-Pilate

MORE INSIDE

Mariamme Caiaphas

Herodias

STILL ONLY 10 SHEKELS!

Herod Berenice
WHY 12 IS A GOOD AGE TO REMARRY

THY-FACE.COM

Simon Peter

 Jesus Christ Peter, it's time for my Transfiguration. Tomorrow I ascend the mountain, and you and the sons of Zebedee shall come with me. I don't have long left now.
🕐 Thursday 11 September 32AD at 4.07pm • Saith • Liketh

 Simon Peter What do you mean, don't have long left now? You're 32! You can finish your mission, then we can retire and enjoy a bit of fishing and anointing!
🕐 Thursday 11 September 32AD at 4.09pm

 Jesus Christ Get thee behind me, Satan! Only kidding! But seriously, what shall it profit a man if he gain the whole world and lose his own soul?
🕐 Thursday 11 September 32AD at 4.12pm

 James the Less Oh, I know – the world!
🕐 Thursday 11 September 32AD at 4.27pm

 James Zebedee He was being rhetorical, dude.
🕐 Thursday 11 September 32AD at 4.29pm

 Simon Peter That was the freakiest night of my life. When we got to the top of the mountain, Jesus turned all white and shiny. Then Moses and Elijah tipped up. And the Holy Ghost appeared and said "this is my son, with which I am well pleased". Jesus, what happened?
🕐 Saturday 13 September 32AD at 12.01pm • Saith • Liketh

 Jesus Christ Jesus? Yes, that is what they called me. Jesus the Grey. Now I am Jesus the White. We meet again, at the turning of the tide.
🕐 Saturday 13 September 32AD at 12.04pm

Simon Peter In one thing you have not changed, my friend. You still talk bollocks!
🕐 Saturday 13 September 32AD at 12.07pm

View Mine Icons (1)

Edit Mine Profile

"The Rock"

Personal Information

Birthday	Status
29 June 1BC	**Married :-(**
Website:	
www.iamarock.gal	

Loggeth out

Friends
Simon Peter hath 212 friends
See all
Find more friends

 Andrew the Fish
 Aretas of Nabatea
 Alcides Heracles
Cypros Phasael

Only one God – but religion still bedevils Pontius Pilate

By Gnaeus Tacitus
Middle East Correspondent

Prior to the occupation, Judea was a powerful ally of Rome, ruled by Herod "don't employ me as a chld minder" the Great. Some of his sons who survived his numerous infanticidal rages still have influence in the region, notably Herod Antipas, axe-happy ruler of Galilee and Samaria.

Although the country is now ruled directly by the Emperor's representative, Pontius "why couldn't they have given me Gaul?" Pilate, some powers still rest with the 71-member 'Sanhedrin', which is similar to our Senate.

There are two main political parties in Judea – the Pharisees (extremely right wing) and the Sadducees (even more right wing). Although the country is so poor it can only afford one God, the Sanhedrin is comprised entirely of priests.

Currently, it is dominated by Sadducees, and the High Priest is Joseph ben Caiaphas, son-in-law of the first High Priest of the occupation, Annas ben Seth (motto: crucify first, ask questions later).

Annas was removed from the High Priesthood in 15AD by the Roman procurator Gratus for his liberal use of capital punishment, possibly the only liberal thing about him. Annas's five sons are all members of the Sanhedrin.

The Pharisee Party is controlled by the cleanliness obsessive Gamaliel ben Simeon, whose son Simon is also a member of the Sanhedrin.

Simon was reputedly healed of leprosy by a travelling conjuror and political activist named Jesus Christ. This Jesus, who is extravagantly popular among the hoi poli, is highly critical of both the Pharisees and Sadducees. Were he to stand in next spring's elections, with his openly Socialist agenda, he and his followers could well gain several seats in the Sanhedrin.

Even more worrying for the priests, Jesus is known to have several anti-Roman Zealots in his following, and a Zealot in the Sanhedrin could well prove too much for Pilate, who might go so far as to disband the ruling council.

The priests have six months to neutralise this Jesus, or else face the possibility of losing their remaining autonomy. The Judean Consulate in Rome advises only travelling to the region if absolutely necessary.

Top to bottom: Herod Antipas, Pontius Pilate, Joseph ben Caiaphas, Jesus Christ.

L

Joseph ben Caiaphas

 Theophilus ben Annas High Priest, my agents report that the Baptist's cousin Jesus has secretly entered Jerusalem for the Feast of the Tabernacles. He fled to Samaria when Herod arrested the Baptist and has been infuriating bakers and winegrowers ever since.
⏱ Wednesday 17 September 32AD at 11:15am • Saith • Liketh

 Inspector Malchus Beggin your pardon sir, e is not ere in secret. At this moment in time e is preaching at the Temple, claiming e was sent by God and that we is all out to nobble him. Permission to proceed there forthwith and seize him by the tabernacles?
⏱ Wednesday 17 September 32AD at 11:18am

 Annas ben Seth I think arresting him will be quite sufficient, officer.
⏱ Wednesday 17 September 32AD at 11:20am

 Joseph ben Caiaphas The sooner we build a bloody great wall around Israel the better! Now, be straight with me – how big a threat is this Jesus?
⏱ Wednesday 17 September 32AD at 11:24am

 Jonathan ben Annas He's a dangerous leftie. Thinks power should be handed over to the meek.
⏱ Wednesday 17 September 32AD at 11:26am

 Theophilus ben Annas He's pretty "meek" himself by all accounts – his best subject at school was woodwork!
⏱ Wednesday 17 September 32AD at 11:28am

 Joseph ben Caiaphas Lol! Maybe we could get him to make his own cross! Save us a shekel or two.
⏱ Wednesday 17 September 32AD at 11:30am

 Annas ben Seth We could try asking him publicly what he thinks of Antipas's marriage to Herodias. Then all we have to do is wait for Antipas to get soused and cut his head off. It worked with the Baptist.
⏱ Wednesday 17 September 32AD at 11:35am

 Joseph of Arimathea But what if Jesus really was sent by God? How embarrassing would that be?
⏱ Wednesday 17 September 32AD at 11:38am

 Joseph ben Caiaphas Lol! Really, Joseph, you're as bad as the Pharisees. You'll believe any old rubbish! Anyway, I've got to go and sacrifice a goat to ensure our sins are forgiven and two lambs to guarantee peace. Malchus, take the guards and bring Jesus in.
⏱ Wednesday 17 September 32AD at 11:40am

View Mine Icons (4)

Edit Mine Profile

High Priest of the Jews

Personal Information

Dwelleth	Status
Jerusalem	**Currently**
Website:	**married**
www.votesadducee.gov.jd	

Proclamations

Temple Slave Insurance

Covers accidental injury, chronic illness and routine beatings.

🖒 Liketh 🖢 Despiseth

Cartoon thyself!

Turn yourself into a cartoon and post it on your ThyFace profile.

🖒 Liketh 🖢 Despiseth

Loggeth out

Friends
Joseph ben Caiaphas hath 94 friends
See all
Find more friends

Pontius Pilate | Jonathan b Annas | Inspector Malchus | Mariamme Caiaphas

Law of Moses cheat sheet

Offence

Punishment

Offence	Punishment
Tell a master you love him	Master shall bore servant's ear through with an awl
Smiteth a man	Death
Curseth a parent	Yes, death
Ox slayeth a man	Ox stoned – to death
Art a witch	Death of witch (plus any cats)
Art a wizard	Stoned to death, breaketh staff
Whore with wizards	Excommunication *check this*
Lieth with a beast	Death (both parties)
Lieth with sibling	Death (both parties)
A priest sinneth	Sacrifice a bullock (not death)
A ruler sinneth	Sacrifice a goat (not death)
Commiteth adultery	Stoned to death
Man rapeth woman	Death (both parties)
Lieth with wife & her mother	All three be burnt (to death, yes)
Lieth with woman fountaining blood	Both excommunicated
Being a false prophet	Death, of course
Blasphemeth	Stoned to death by everyone
Man lieth with man	Take a wild stab –
Sacrifice to other God	Totally f---ing obliterated

THY-FACE.COM

Jesus Christ

 John Zebedee Hey, new Jesus. You're much cooler than the old Jesus! James just told me about when the Temple guards came to arrest you. You commanded fire to rain down from Heaven and consume them, just like Elijah did, or someone. I wish I'd seen it!
🕐 Wednesday 17 September 32AD at 3.37pm • Saith • Liketh

 Jesus Christ I did no such thing. Your brother's winding you up! Again!
🕐 Wednesday 17 September 32AD at 3:40pm

 Mary Magdalene Didn't you do any smiting at all?
🕐 Wednesday 17 September 32AD at 3:42pm

 Jesus Christ Well, I did have to raise my voice a bit at one point.
🕐 Wednesday 17 September 32AD at 3:43pm

 Theophilus ben Annas Jesus. May I welcome you to Jerusalem. I understand you have been preaching the scriptures, and I wonder whether you might be able to help us on a question of the Law. Earlier today, we seized this woman in the act of adultery. Moses says we should stone her to death. What do you think?
🕐 Wednesday 17 September 32AD at 4.29pm • Saith • Liketh

 John Zebedee The Jezza! She told me she was single!
🕐 Wednesday 17 September 32AD at 4.30pm

 Jesus Christ John, please! If she is to be stoned, then he who is without sin should cast the first stone.
🕐 Wednesday 17 September 32AD at 4.32pm

 Theophilus ben Annas Very droll! We'd never stone anyone if that were the Law!
🕐 Wednesday 17 September 32AD at 4.34pm

View Mine Icons (31)

Edit Mine Profile

The Saviour

Personal Information

Birthday	Status
25 December	**Watch this space!**

Website:
www.bornagaininme.il

Proclamations

Make your thyPhone count

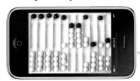

Thousands of new apps for your thyPhone, including this state-of-the-art digital scientific abacus.

👍 Liketh 👎 Despiseth

Immaculate connections

Sign up for Virgin Broadband. Endorsed by the Messiah's mum!

👍 Liketh 👎 Despiseth

Loggeth out

Friends
Jesus Christ hath 50143 friends
See all
Find more friends

 Claudia Pilate

 Eunice Lois

 Dorcas Tabitha

Priscilla Aquila

TOP SECRET

T.B.ANNAS
DIRECTOR
MOSSAD

John Zebedee – whoring

John Mark & "friend"

№ 45638778K

"APOSTLES" OF JESUS CHRIST

Judas Iscariot – dicing

Simon Zelotes – smiting person unknown

Matthew Levi – tax evasion

Mary Mag[...]

Theophilus ben Annas

 Joseph ben Caiaphas What in God's name is going on, Theo? You had this Jesus, but he gave you the slip?
🕛 Thursday 18 September 32AD at 9:21am • Saith • Liketh

 Theophilus ben Annas He beguiled Malchus and the Temple guards, so I tried the old adulterous woman routine, but he'd obviously heard it before.
🕛 Thursday 18 September 32AD at 9:25am

 Annas ben Seth Has he never clipped the edge of his beard? Or eaten a lobster? In my day, we'd have arrested him first and trumped up the charges later.
🕛 Thursday 18 September 32AD at 9:31am

 Jonathan ben Annas Arresting him now could prove dangerous. Too many halfwits believe he's the Messiah. We need to take him when he's alone.
🕛Thursday 18 September 32AD at 9:32am

 Joseph ben Caiaphas And how do we do that, pray?
🕛 Thursday 18 September 32AD at 9:34am

 Theophilus ben Annas Through his apostles. I've been reviewing their security files – a ragbag of Zealots, womanisers and at least one ass-coverer. Malchus took this icon while Jesus was allegedly healing a blind man. You'll see the one called John Zebedee appears to be picking the blind man's pocket.
🕛 Thursday 18 September 32AD at 9:36am

 Joseph ben Caiaphas Who's the rather shifty looking character in the top left-hand corner?
🕛 Thursday 18 September 32AD at 9:41am

 Theophilus ben Annas That's Judas Iscariot, an ex-scribe. I'm keeping a close eye on him. Don't worry, we'll nail this Jesus one way or the other.
🕛 Thursday 18 September 32AD at 9:45am

View Mine Icons (1)

Edit Mine Profile

Priest and Director of Mossad

Personal Information

Birthday	Status
Classified	**Classified**

Website:
www.votesadducee.gov.jd

Proclamations

Weekends in Babylon

Getting married? Come to the party city for your stag night!

👍 Liketh 🖐 Despiseth

Wife obedience classes

Help your wife become a great companion – we guarantee fast and lasting results.

👍 Liketh 🖐 Despiseth

Loggeth out

VOTE SADDUCEE!

Tough on sin! Tough on the causes of sin! In fact... tough on everything!

THY-FACE.COM

Nicodemus ben Gurion

 Simon the Pharisee Hey, Nico. I'm getting serious grief from the Sadducees. The Ben Annas brothers have been asking me how well I know Jesus. If he isn't the Son of God, we're in deep do-do.
🕐 Wednesday 26 November 32ᴀᴅ at 7:30pm • Saith • Liketh

 Nicodemus ben Gurion Well, let's deny all knowledge of him. Jehovah will forgive us. lol!
🕐 Wednesday 26 November 32ᴀᴅ at 7:35pm

 Simon the Pharisee Be serious! The problem is, it's impossible to get a straight answer out of Jesus.
🕐 Wednesday 26 November 32ᴀᴅ at 7:37pm

 Nicodemus ben Gurion Tell me about it. The other day he said "love thy neighbour as thyself", so I asked him what exactly constituted a neighbour. Do they have to live next door or whatever, and he answered with this interminable story about a bad priest and a good Samaritan and a man who got robbed. None of us had the first clue what he was talking about.
🕐 Wednesday 26 November 32ᴀᴅ at 7:40pm

 Simon the Pharisee You're going to have to ask him straight who his dad is. That's all there is to it.
🕐 Wednesday 26 November 32ᴀᴅ at 7:43pm

 Jesus Christ Hi Nicodemus. Are you coming to Andrew's birthday party on Sunday?
🕐 Wednesday 26 November 32ᴀᴅ at 7:52pm • Saith • Liketh

 Nicodemus ben Gurion Will there be fish? I'm joking. Listen, if I ask you a question, will you give me a straight answer? Are you truly the Son of God?
🕐 Wednesday 26 November 32ᴀᴅ at 8:02pm

 Jesus Christ Nicodemus, if healing 2000 lepers, 71 visual impaired people and reanimating the dead hasn't convinced you, I'm sure me saying, "by the way, I'm the Son of God" won't do the trick.
🕐 Wednesday 26 November 32ᴀᴅ at 8:04pm

 Nicodemus ben Gurion No need to get sarcastic.
🕐 Wednesday 26 November 32ᴀᴅ at 8:06pm

 James the Less So is he or isn't he? I didn't catch it.
🕐 Wednesday 26 November 32ᴀᴅ at 10:14pm

 John Zebedee Dude, you are such a retard.
🕐 Wednesday 26 November 32ᴀᴅ at 10:17pm

View Mine Icons (6)

Edit Mine Profile

Priest and Pharisee

Personal Information

Birthday	Father
3 August	Gurion

Website:
www.votepharisee.gal

Proclamations

Foods not to eat

For they art an abomination! How to eat without being smited!

👍 Liketh ✋ Despiseth

The secret of white teeth!

Thought your camel couldn't be more attractive? Think again!

👍 Liketh ✋ Despiseth

Loggeth out

Friends
Nicodemus ben Gurion hath 112 friends
See all
Find more friends

 Joseph of Arimathea

 Gamaliel b Simeon

 Johanan b Zakkai

 Simon b Nathaneal

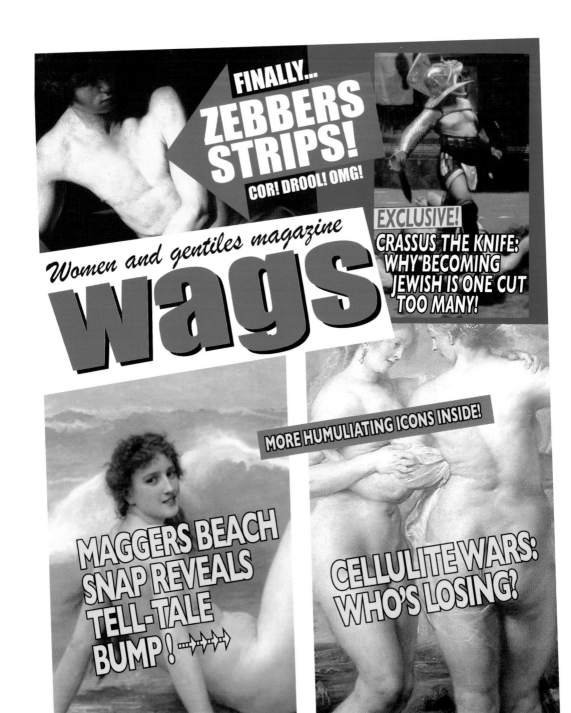

THY-FACE.COM

John Zebedee

✍ John Zebedee hath taken the test Who Art The Greatest Apostle?

 Jesus Christ John, do you not know that in the Kingdom of Heaven he who is first is the least, and he who is last is the greatest?
🕐 Thursday 27 November 32AD at 10:35am • Saith • Liketh

 John Zebedee Excellent! I came 12th.
🕐 Thursday 27 November 32AD at 10:38am.

 Mary Magdalene John Mark styled my hair! Isn't it fab?
🕐 Thursday 27 November 32AD at 12:40pm • Saith • Liketh

 John Mark OMG! You should have seen it before! Whoever cut it last time should be crucified!
🕐 Thursday 27 November 32AD at 12:59pm

 Jesus Christ Excuse me! I cut it last time.
🕐 Thursday 27 November 32AD at 1:19pm

 Mary Magdalene Hey Zebbers. Can't you persuade Jesus to come home? Pleeeeeease!! Lazarus has changed his status to Really Very Poorly Indeed and he's simply desperate to be healed!
🕐 Saturday 29 November 32AD at 8:44pm • Saith • Liketh

 Joanna Chuza He's not the only Magdalene desperate for a "laying on of hands" from Jesus!
🕐 Saturday 29 November 32AD at 8:45pm

 James Zebedee Relax. I'll tell him. It's not as if anything's going to happen to Sick Boy, is it? I can tell when someone's fakin' it. And Lazarus is definitely fakin' it.
🕐 Saturday 29 November 32AD at 9:01pm

☠ Lazarus Magdalene's status hath changed to Dead • Saith • Liketh

---

View Mine Icons (19619)

Edit Mine Profile

> **Top Apostle and Rock Star**

Personal Information

Birthday	Status
27 December	**Single & lovin' it!**

Website:
www.planetzebedee.com

Proclamations

Meet Celtic slaves today

Guaranteed no chatting!

👍 Liketh 👎 Despiseth

Ultimate rock star rides

African racing zebra with go-faster stripes. Available in two colours.

👍 Liketh 👎 Despiseth

Friends)
John Zebedee hath 64122 friends
See all
Find more friends

 Herod Berenice

 50 Shekel

 Drusilla Cleopatra

 James Zebedee

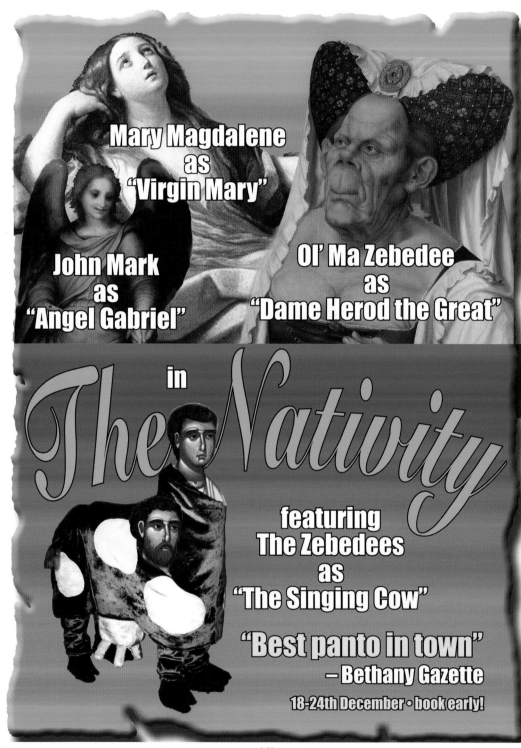

Mary Magdalene
as
"Virgin Mary"

John Mark
as
"Angel Gabriel"

Ol' Ma Zebedee
as
"Dame Herod the Great"

in

The Nativity

featuring
The Zebedees
as
"The Singing Cow"

"Best panto in town"
– Bethany Gazette

18-24th December • book early!

Mary Magdalene

 John Zebedee Of course, we all knew he was ill. It was just a matter of time. I wish I could have done something.
🕐 Wednesday 3 December 32AD at 11:28pm • Saith • Liketh

 Mary Magdalene If only Jesus had been here!
🕐 Wednesday 3 December 32AD at 11:29pm

 John Zebedee Well, we're on our way now. If you or Martha need someone to comfort and console you, I'd be only too happy. I know how vulnerable you must be feeling right now.
🕐 Wednesday 3 December 32AD at 11:32pm

 James Zebedee You are so selfless, dude.
🕐 Wednesday 3 December 32AD at 11:33pm

 Martha Magdalene Yes, it's very good of you to come. If Jesus performs one of his magic tricks at the funeral, it'll really take the edge off what might otherwise have been a very unhappy occasion.
🕐 Wednesday 3 December 32AD at 11:39pm

 Jesus Christ Martha, Martha. Why art thou troubled? Lazarus isn't dead, he's merely sleeping.
🕐 Wednesday 3 December 32AD at 11:48pm

 Doubting Thomas That's right, he always kips on his back with his legs in the air!
🕐 Wednesday 3 December 32AD at 11:50pm

 Joanna Chuza He's been dead for four days. Even the flies are wearing nose pegs.
🕐 Wednesday 3 December 32AD at 11:51pm

 John Zebedee Oh ye of little faith! If Jesus says he's only sleeping, he's only sleeping. Besides, Lazarus always smelt like a goat in a fish tank. No offence.
🕐 Wednesday 3 December 32AD at 11:53pm

 Martha Magdalene And I suppose John the Baptist only had a shaving cut?
🕐 Wednesday 3 December 32AD at 11:55pm

 Lazarus Magdalene Where am I? It's dark in here. Let me out! God, I stinketh!
🕐 Wednesday 3 December 32AD at 12:00pm • Saith • Liketh

HATH COME TO PASS
☙ Lazarus Magdalene's status hath changed to Risen • Saith • Liketh

---

View Mine Icons (453)
Edit Mine Profile

Jesus loves me best!

Personal Information

Birthday | Status
22 July | It's complicated
Website:
www.ilovejesus.jd

Proclamations

Play as a Geek Goddess!

ZEALOT WARS

👍 Liketh 👎 Despiseth

Tired of being snubbed?

When it comes to noses, big is beautiful. Bronzino's Rhinoplasty.

👍 Liketh 👎 Despiseth

Loggeth out

TEMPUS

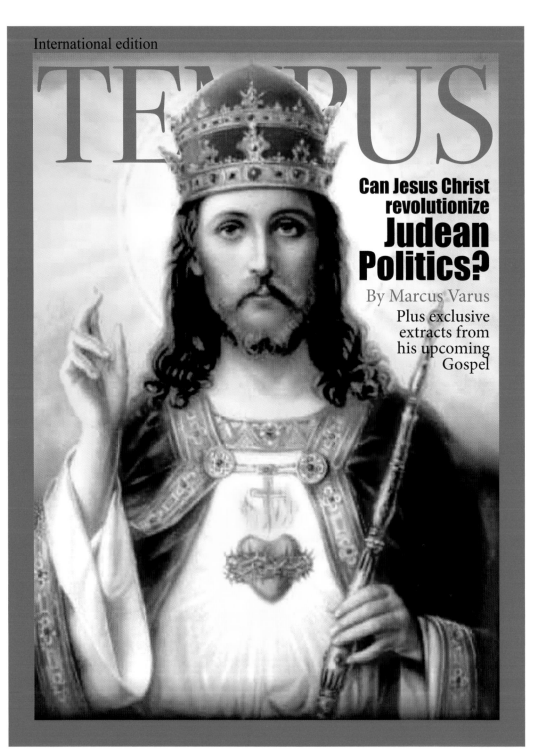

Can Jesus Christ revolutionize Judean Politics?

By Marcus Varus

Plus exclusive extracts from his upcoming Gospel

Jesus Christ

 Joseph of Arimathea I know the other Sadducees are smitten by the Moneychangers, but I hate them as much as you do. Attack them again, and I'll see the rabble's behind you. Holidays are approaching anyway, so most of them will be juiced up and itching for a rumble.
⏱ Monday 2 March 33AD at 10:23am • Saith • Liketh

 Jesus Christ Joseph, thou art truly close to the Kingdom of Heaven.
⏱ Monday 2 March 33AD at 10:25am

 Joseph of Arimathea Whatever. Now listen, you need to ride into Jerusalem on a young ass to fulfil the prophesy. Send a couple of your cronies to get mine from the Mount Olive Stables in Bethphage – the password is "the Lord hath need of it."
⏱ Monday 2 March 33AD at 10:28am

 Jesus Christ OK, I need two volunteers to go and pick me up a young ass in Bethphage.
⏱ Monday 2 March 33AD at 11:00am • Saith • Liketh

 John Mark Ooh! Me! Me! Me! Me! Me!
⏱ Monday 2 March 33AD at 11:01am

 James Zebedee Well, that wasn't at all predictable.
⏱ Monday 2 March 33AD at 11:02am

 Simon Zelotes At last! We finally kicked some moneychanging ass! Great accompanying song by the way, Zebedees. "Hosanna! Hosanna! You're going home on a medical donkey cart!"
⏱ Monday 2 March 33AD at 6:15pm • Saith • Liketh

 Matthew Levi How many people do you reckon were with us? The Temple guards say it was only half a multitude, but I reckon it was at least two!
⏱ Monday 2 March 33AD at 6:20pm

John Zebedee Jesus was supercool. "My house is a house of prayer, yet ye have made it a den of thieves, you pug-faced moneygrabbing tosspots!"
⏱ Monday 2 March 33AD at 6:23pm

James Zebedee No way did Jesus say that, dude.
⏱ Monday 2 March 33AD at 6:25pm

View Mine Icons (33)
Edit Mine Profile

Behold the Me!

Personal Information

Birthday
25 December

Website:
www.bornagaininme.il

Status
Thinking of settling down

Loggeth out

Friends
Jesus Christ hath 64551 friends
See all
Find more friends

 Veronica Berenice
 James Christ
 Mariamme Caiaphas
 Apostle Philip

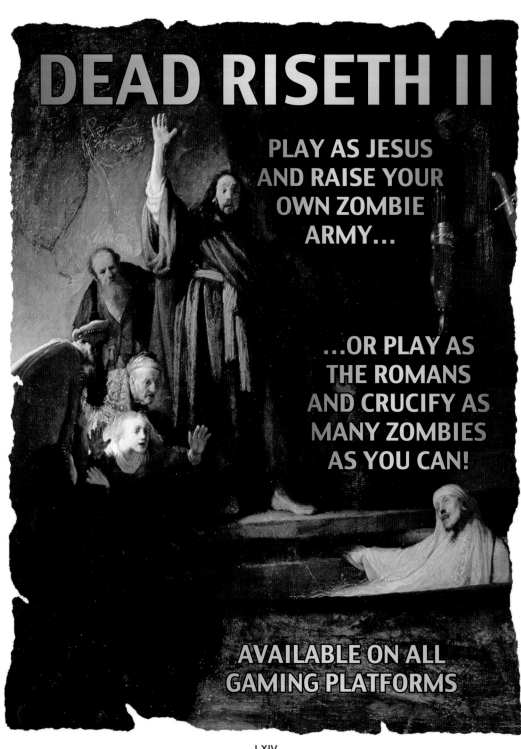

THY-FACE.COM

Joseph ben Caiaphas

 Inspector Malchus I must express my deep regret at the events what occured in the Temple yesterday afternoon. I pursued the suspect Jesus through the multitudes towards the entrance, where I endeavoured to arrest him. But I there encountered one of his Apostles, who proceeded to kick me hard in the left vestibule.
🕐 Tuesday 3 March 33AD at 4:21pm • Saith • Liketh

> Joseph ben Caiaphas It brings tears to my eyes just hearing about it, Inspector.
> 🕐 Tuesday 3 March 33AD at 4:22pm

 Gamaliel ben Simeon Caiaphas! What are you doing about this Jesus? He's raising a zombie army to go alongside his human multitudes! When he was only attacking the Moneychangers, he was fine – even if that John Zebedee did put a whoopie cushion on my seat in the Sanhedrin. But sooner or later, Jesus is going to upset the Romans, and it'll be hammer time for all of us.
🕐 Tuesday 17 March 33AD at 6:00pm • Saith • Liketh

> Theophilus ben Annas But Gamaliel, Jesus has prominent supporters among your Pharisees, including Nicodemus ben Gurion and your own son, Simon.
> 🕐 Tuesday 17 March 33AD at 6:08am

> Gamaliel ben Simeon What about your Sadducees? Your "man of the people" Joseph of Arimathea supplied him with a brand new sports donkey!
> 🕐 Tuesday 17 March 33AD at 6:10pm

> Annas ben Seth I don't understand why Jesus is so popular – his policies are preposterous. He says that divorce is against God and people should marry for life. But my latest wife is nearly 19. I must be allowed to trade her in soon – I've had her nearly six years.
> 🕐 Tuesday 17 March 33AD at 6:12am

> Joseph ben Caiaphas It's obvious we have to work together to "remove" this Jesus. For the good of the people! He's bound to return to Jerusalem for the Passover, but we can't take him openly or we'll have a riot on our hands. Fortunately, Theophilus has a plan, and all your Pharisees need to do is give us support when we ask for it. 😈 Evil lol!
> 🕐 Tuesday 17 March 33AD at 6:16am

View Mine Icons (4)
Edit Mine Profile

High Priest of the Jews

Personal Information

Dwelleth
Jerusalem

Religion
Take a guess

Website:
www.votesadducee.gov.jd

Proclamations

Predict the weather!

View and analyse a wide range of entrails with the latest Weather Prediction app for your thyPhone.

👍 Liketh 👎 Despiseth

Looking for a new wife?

We psychologically evaluate all our clients to find women who are guaranteed 100% compliant.

👍 Liketh 👎 Despiseth

Loggeth out

Friends
Joseph ben Caiaphas hath 94 friends
See all
Find more friends

Joseph of Arimathea   Annas ben Seth   Gamaliel b Simeon   Herod Antipas

CIRCUSMAXIMUS

circusmaximus.co.jd

WINTER OLYMPICS LATEST

Only 2000 snow leopards slaughtered this year, say disappointed spectators

FULL STORY PAGE 12

Judah ben Hur takes bookies for a ride

Ben Hur 1 Messala 0

Bookies' favourite Messala crushed in arena as Jew romps to victory.

FULL STORY
Pages 3, 4 & 7

TODAY'S RESULTS INSIDE: LIONS VS GIRAFFES • DONKEY CLUBBING

How many women will be slaughtered in the upcoming Amazon Games?

Guess the correct number and win! win! win!
We guarantee the best odds!

THY-FACE.COM

Judas Iscariot

◆ Judas Iscariot lost his 900th consecutive game of Tarsus Hold 'Em Poker, but he can still win a thyPod Touch • Saith • Liketh

187 more similar stories

View Mine Icons (2)

Edit Mine Profile

Educated Apostle

 Matthew Levi Judas, I've just been conducting a routine audit of our financial affairs, and cash reserves appear to be down by a substantial amount – around 30 pieces of silver. The only place I can think it could be is in your float. You don't hold that much, do you?

⏱ Thursday 19 March 33AD at 8:01am • Saith • Liketh

Personal Information

Birthday	Status
31 October	**Looking**

Website:
www.judesbettingtips.il

 Judas Iscariot Maybe. Yeah, possibly. I dunno. Sounds about right. I'll get back to you.
⏱ Thursday 19 March 33AD at 8:13am

 Matthew Levi No hurry. After Passover will do.
⏱ Thursday 19 March 33AD at 8:15am

 Judas Iscariot When we were round Simon's last night, a receipt fell out of Mary Magdalene's handbag for the ointment she used to anoint Jesus's feet while Martha cooked dinner. 300 denarii! I don't see why I can't sell that to help the poor, just because a certain "someone" gets a good "anointing" once in a while.

⏱ Thursday 19 March 33AD at 10:37am • Saith • Liketh

 Jesus Christ Judas, it's laudable you want to help the poor, but you can help them after I'm gone. Mary bought this to anoint my body for the grave.
⏱ Thursday 19 March 33AD at 10:43am

 John Zebedee You are into some seriously kinky shit, dude. Respect.
⏱ Thursday 19 March 33AD at 10:44am

 Satan Ah Judas. I wanted to speak to you personally as you've been such a good client. It's about your application for a further 30 pieces of silver credit at the casino. I'm afraid it's been declined. Nothing to do with me – we use an external credit reference agency. I do have a suggestion, though. Have a word with the priest Theophilus ben Annas. I'm sure he'll help.

⏱ Thursday 19 March 33AD at 11:25am • Saith • Liketh

Proclamations

In debt? Hock your soul!

Warning: not all souls can be redeemed.

👍 Liketh 👎 Despiseth

Hoping to make a fast buck?

Get 10 shekels ABSOLUTELY FREE the first time you play 666.com online bingo. No deposit required.

👍 Liketh 👎 Despiseth

Loggeth out

Friends
Judas Iscariot hath 19 friends
See all
Find more friends

 Jesus Christ   Matthew Levi   Simon Zelotes   Satan

LXVII

VOTE PHARISEE

GAMALIEL BEN SIMEON

TOGETHER WE CAN MAKE A CLEAN START

SANHEDRIN ELECTIONS • 9 APRIL
VOTE • THEN WASH YOUR HANDS

YES WE* CAN

*EXCLUDES WOMEN AND GENTILES

Jesus Christ

 John Zebedee So what we doing for the feast tonight? I could slaughter a Passover Lamb Vindaloo.
🕐 Thursday 19 March 33AD at 2:31pm • Saith • Liketh

 Doubting Thomas There's no way we'll find an Indian in Jerusalem now. The place is swarming with tourists. We should have booked weeks ago.
🕐 Thursday 19 March 33AD at 2:34pm

 James the Less Yes, did anyone else spot how busy it was when we entered town today?
🕐 Thursday 19 March 33AD at 2:39pm

 Simon Peter What – you mean the thousands of people lining the streets, throwing palm branches in our path and shouting, "Hosanna: Blessed is the King of Israel that cometh in the name of the Lord"? Anyone else notice it, or was it just me and Sherlock?
🕐 Thursday 19 March 33AD at 2:41pm

 Jesus Christ John and Peter – could you pop down and confirm our booking for tonight at the Ascetic Arms?
🕐 Thursday 19 March 33AD at 3:01pm • Saith • Liketh

 Jude Thaddeus The Ascetic Arms? Are you kidding? They only serve bread and water.
🕐 Thursday 19 March 33AD at 3:03pm

 James Zebedee Don't sweat it, dude. As long as we have Jesus and an urn of water, we're cushtie.
🕐 Thursday 19 March 33AD at 3:05pm

 John Zebedee They do poppadoms, surely?
🕐 Thursday 19 March 33AD at 3:06pm

 Andrew the Fish Seriously, if they don't do fish, it's the last supper I'm going to.
🕐 Thursday 19 March 33AD at 3:08pm

 Jesus Christ You guys! Look, here's the plan. We stay at the Ascetic Arms until midnight, then we sneak out of the city to the Garden of Gethsemane. I want to have a chat with me dad, and it's the only chance we'll have to get away from the multitude.
🕐 Thursday 19 March 33AD at 3:11pm

 Judas Iscariot So where exactly is this garden?
🕐 Thursday 19 March 33AD at 3:13pm

View Mine Icons (34)

Edit Mine Profile

Messiah of the Jews

Personal Information

Birthday
25 December

Status
Don't ask

Website:
www.bornagaininme.il

Loggeth out

Friends
Jesus Christ hath 64424 friends
See all
Find more friends

 Simon Peter
 John Mark
 Jude Christ
Claudia Pilate

Thank you for choosing the

Ascetic Arms

for your Passover meal
We trust you didn't enjoy
your supper here too much
and that it won't be your last!

NOT ALL KISSES
ARE WELCOME

THY-FACE.COM

Mary Magdalene

 John Zebedee hath poked Mary Magdalene • Saith • Liketh

Mary Magdalene hath fervently denied it • Saith • Liketh

Mary Magdalene How's your lads night out, Zebbers? You still on the raz with my main man Jesus?
🕐 Friday 20 March 33AD at 12:39am • Saith • Liketh

 John Zebedee I wish! JC has come to some God-forsaken garden to have a chinwag with his old man – not the dead one, the one that "art in Heaven". He told me and Peter to stay awake, but we've had too much vino. Peter's already snoring like a moose.
🕐 Friday 20 March 33AD at 12:42am

 Mary Magdalene So how was the meal?
🕐 Friday 20 March 33AD at 12:45am

 John Zebedee Bit freaky. Jesus came in wearing only a towel, and insisted on washing our feet. I think he'd already been at the urn! He did his breaking the bread trick with his roll and passed it round, saying "eateth of my body" – you know, in that voice he does. Then he passed round a grail of Chateau Jesus and said "drinketh of my blood, which I hath shed for you", or words to that effect. Hold on, I can see Peter coming round…
🕐 Friday 20 March 33AD at 12:50am

 Simon Peter Did you tell her what he said to me? He said he was going out, and I said, "can I come?" "Verily, verily," he says, "the cock shall not crow till thou hast denied me thrice!" What's that all about?
🕐 Friday 20 March 33AD at 12:52am

 Mary Magdalene He's under a lot of stress, bless him. I'll bring my oil round tomorrow and give him a good anointing. That usually does the trick. And you can tell that creep Judas Iscariot to keep well clear of me!
🕐 Friday 20 March 33AD at 12:54am

 John Zebedee I'm feeling a bit stressed myself. How do you fancy popping over with your ointment now?
🕐 Friday 20 March 33AD at 12:56am

Simon Peter John! Put your weapon away and get your sword out! Someone's coming! It's Judas, and he's brought the Temple guards with him!
🕐 Friday 20 March 33AD at 12:59am

View Mine Icons (460)

Edit Mine Profile

Jesus loves me more than you!

Personal Information

Birthday
22 July

Status
Going steady – sort of

Website:
www.ilovejesus.jd

Proclamations

Bethany Finishing School

We offer courses in homemaking and going forth and multiplying.

👍 Liketh 👎 Despiseth

Sex your unborn baby

Our home testing kits include full instructions and sacrificial chicken.

👍 Liketh 👎 Despiseth

Loggeth out

Friends
Mary Magdalene hath 13555 friends
See all
Find more friends

 John Zebedee

 Joanna Chuza

 James Zebedee

Susanna Myrbarer

🏛 TEMPLE GUARDS INCIDENT REPORT

AFFIX ICON HERE

At precisely 1:32 in the A.M. in the premature hours of
Friday 20th of March last, myself and officers of the
Temple Guard accompanied by his holy personage Theophilus
ben Annas proceeded in an orderly manner to the Garden
of Gethsemane in the vicisitude of the Mount of Olives,
acting on information obfuscated from the supergrass
Judas Iscariot, it being our intention to apprehend
the celebrated felon, Jesus Christ, who it was our
understanding was up to no good in the flowery region.

Having arrived at the said location, Judas Iscariot
identified the suspect by means of a predemented signal
comprising a kiss to the cheeky area. It was at this
junction that a particularly ugly apostle drew his sword
and lopped off my ear, exposing it to all and sundries.

When his holiness confronted the felon Jesus Christ with
details of his trespasses, he replied, "it's a fair cop,
guv. You got me bang to rights. I done it all right and
no mistake." The rest of the gang then made off with my
earhole, while we proceeded to take Jesus up the Annas

[continued]

Signed.... *Inspector Malchus* .... Date. 21 March 33AD ....

James the Less

 James the Less Where is everyone? What's happened? I don't like the dark! I want my mum!
🕐 Friday 20 March 33AD at 2:33am • Saith • Liketh

 Simon Peter "What's happened"!!? Where are you?
🕐 Friday 20 March 33AD at 2:35am

 James the Less I'm in the garden. I fell asleep and when I woke up you'd all gone and left me!
🕐 Friday 20 March 33AD at 2:37pm

 Simon Peter You mean you slept through the fight? The Temple guards came and arrested Jesus!
🕐 Friday 20 March 33AD at 2:38am

 Simon Zelotes Peter cut off their leader's ear with his sword – it was rockin'.
🕐 Friday 20 March 33AD at 2:40am

 Simon Peter We were betrayed by that bastard Judas Iscariot. I wish I knew where he was now!
🕐 Friday 20 March 33AD at 2:42am

 Simon Zelotes 🐍 He's met with an unfortunate accident. Apparently, he was climbing a tree when he accidentally hanged himself. I saw it happen!
🕐 Friday 20 March 33AD at 2:47am

 Mary Magdalene Screw Judas! What about Jesus?
🕐 Friday 20 March 33AD at 2:48am

 John Zebedee They've taken him to the priest's house. I'm hiding behind the curtains now. They've put him on trial, but Jesus is running rings round the Banana Brothers. They want to execute him, but are too scared and want the Romans to do it. *sent from my thyPhone*
🕐 Friday 20 March 33AD at 2:50am

 Josephus ben Matthias Hi, I work for the Mail on Sabbath. I'm told you guys know Jesus?
🕐 Friday 20 March 33AD at 3:29am • Saith • Liketh

 Simon Peter Once, twice, three times. That's a lie!
🕐 Friday 20 March 33AD at 3:29am

 ThyFace Alarm Cockerel Cock-a-doodle-doo!
🕐 Friday 20 March 33AD at 3:30am

John Zebedee You are so not gonna live that down!
🕐 Friday 20 March 33AD at 3:31am

View Mine Icons (12)

Edit Mine Profile

James the 'Less than the full shekel'. Note: this account has been facejacked by JZ. lol!

Personal Information

Birthday	Status
3 May	**Single!**

Website:
www.imachumofjesus.il

Proclamations

Play Petting Zoo online!

Waste your life raising pointless animals you can't eat.

👍 Liketh 👎 Despiseth

Egghead? Test your IQ now!

Beat your previous score of 12!

👍 Liketh 👎 Despiseth

Loggeth out

Friends
James the Less hath 3122 friends
See all
Find more friends

 Virgin Mary

Jesus Christ

Jude Thaddeus

 Ol' Ma Zebedee

roman expat

magazine

WE RATE THE BEST SLAVE MARKETS OUTSIDE ROME

3000 THINGS NEVER TO EAT IN JUDEA

RELAXING WITH GAIUS CALIGULA

CHARIOTS FOR HIRE: TEST-DRIVING THE NEW COUPES

Pontius Pilate

HATH COME TO PASS

 Joseph ben Caiaphas **hath poked Pontius Pilate** • Saith • Liketh

 Pontius Pilate It's four o'clock in the soddin' morning! This better be good, old man, otherwise I'm looking at a cross with your name on it!
⏱ Friday 20 March 33AD at 3:58am • Saith • Liketh

 Joseph ben Caiaphas Yes, it is rather urgent. We have a dangerous terrorist in custody and we feel he should be crucified straight away, before the mob wakes up.
⏱ Friday 20 March 33AD at 4:00am

 Pontius Pilate I see. Another political opponent the Ministry of Religious Tolerance wants "disappearing". What's this one supposed to have done?
⏱ Friday 20 March 33AD at 4:01am

 Annas ben Seth He's a villain, obviously. Otherwise we wouldn't have brought him to you.
⏱ Friday 20 March 33AD at 4:03am

 Pontius Pilate Then try him yourself and let me get back to sleep. If the missus wakes up, you're history.
⏱ Friday 20 March 33AD at 4:05am

 Inspector Malchus Beggin your pardon, guv, but e's a dangerous criminal. Claims e's King of the Jews. When I tried to arrest him, one of his followers cut off my ear. Now my helmet don't fit properly.
⏱ Friday 20 March 33AD at 4:08am

 Pontius Pilate All right, log him on. Now, criminal, are they telling the truth? Do you claim to be King?
⏱ Friday 20 March 33AD at 4:10am

 Jesus Christ My kingdom is not of this world. I was born to bear witness to the truth.
⏱ Friday 20 March 33AD at 4:11am

 Pontius Pilate Truth! In this place? lol! I've read about this man, Caiaphas. He's clearly simple. Let him go.
⏱ Friday 20 March 33AD at 4:12am

 Joseph ben Caiaphas But he claims he's King of the Jews! It's an insult to the Emperor! He's been stirring up trouble in Galilee for years. You must do something!
⏱ Friday 20 March 33AD at 4:14am

Pontius Pilate In Galilee? Why didn't you say? That's Herod's country. Let Herod deal with him. lol.
⏱ Friday 20 March 33AD at 4:16am

View Mine Icons (36)

Edit Mine Profile

Roman Governor of Judea

Personal Information

Birthday	Status
25 June	**Married to**
Website:	**Claudia Procula**
www.governorofjudea.gov.rm	

Proclamations

You can't lose with property

Pompeii: stunning views *and* a fantastic investment opportunity.

👍 Liketh 🗡 Despiseth

Bob's Crucifixion Supplies

Hang 'em high, for low, low prices!

👍 Liketh 🗡 Despiseth

Loggeth out

Friends
Pontius Pilate hath 316 friends
See all
Find more friends

 Gaius Caligula

 Emperor Tiberius

 Claudia Pilate

 Joseph b Caiaphas

WANTED

B. A. BARABBAS – FOR
TEMPLE BANK ROBBERY
AND GENERAL ZEALOTRY

THY-FACE.COM

Herod Antipas

HATH COME TO PASS

 Joseph ben Caiaphas **hath poked Herod Antipas** • Saith • Liketh

 Herod Antipas Caiaphas, old man. Good God! Is that the time? I must have slept all day! I'm due to start drinking again in five minutes. Hang on – is it still morning? Why the hell are you poking me at this time?
⏱ Friday 20 March 33AD at 6:15am • Saith • Liketh

 Joseph ben Caiaphas Stop ranting and sharpen your axe. I have another head for you to liberate.
⏱ Friday 20 March 33AD at 6:18am

 Herod Antipas Ha-bloody-ha. If his head feels anything like mine, he'd welcome it. Why don't you do it yourself?
⏱ Friday 20 March 33AD at 6:20am

 Joseph ben Caiaphas I would, but he works out of Galilee, and Pilate thinks you should deal with it.
⏱ Friday 20 March 33AD at 6:21am

 Herod Antipas You mean you asked Pilate and he said no? What's is this, Operation Hot Potato?
⏱ Friday 20 March 33AD at 6:24am

 Joseph ben Caiaphas His name's Jesus. He's a cousin of your old pal, John the Baptist.
⏱ Friday 20 March 33AD at 6:23am

 Herod Antipas Oh, thank you. We need to execute the most popular man since Moses, so we'll get Herod to do it. Like I'm not unpopular enough. Let me think about it and get back to you.
⏱ Friday 20 March 33AD at 6:26am

HATH COME TO PASS

 Herod Antipas **hath poked** Pontius Pilate • Saith • Liketh

Pontius Pilate Don't tell me. You're too yellow to execute the hippy for the beardies? Honestly, when Herod the Great was strangling his useless children, where were you hiding? Still, it's not in my interest to upset the priests or the plebs, so I'll save your neck. I'll agree to crucify Jesus, which will get the God Squad off our backs, then, as it's Passover, I'll agree to release a prisoner to the mob. They'll say Jesus, I'll have to let him go, and there'll be no riot. It's a plan that can't possibly fail.
⏱ Friday 20 March 33AD at 7:01 am • Saith • Liketh

View Mine Icons (22)

Edit Mine Profile

Ruler of Galilee and Perea

Personal Information

Status
Married to Herodias

Website:
www.ethnarchofgalilee.gov.gal

Proclamations

Endangered species

Join the Galilee Hunt and enjoy a fun day out butchering them.

◻ Liketh 🗨 Despiseth

Vote Zealot in Galilee!

Kick out Herod Antipas now!

◻ Liketh 🗨 Despiseth

Loggeth out

Friends
Herod Antipas hath 413 friends
See all
Find more friends

 Herodias   Chuza the Steward   Joseph b Caiaphas   Herod Agrippa

THY-FACE.COM

B A Barabbas

 B A Barabbas Listen up, fools! Unless you can bust me outta jail, I got exactly 44 minutes plus ads before the Romans crucify my ass for a crime I didn't commit!
🕐 Friday 20 March 33AD at 8:01am • Saith • Liketh

View Mine Icons (144)

Edit Mine Profile

Camel engineer extraordinaire

Personal Information

Dwelleth
At the Emperor's pleasure

Website:
www.bad-attitude.jd

Proclamations

Need a fake passport?

 Colonel Hannibal Don't worry, we'll ram the prison walls with my elephants and make good our escape.
🕐 Friday 20 March 33AD at 8:02am

 B A Barabbas I ain't gittin on no elephant.
🕐 Friday 20 March 33AD at 8:03am

 The Face Why do we need to break him out at all? Pilate will offer to release a prisoner for Passover. We just have to make sure it's B A.
🕐 Friday 20 March 33AD at 8:05am

 Colonel Hannibal Nah! That won't work. The crowd'll vote for Jesus. He's far more popular.
🕐 Friday 20 March 33AD at 8:06am

 Mad Dog Not unless we can somehow switch the real crowd for our own crowd!
🕐 Friday 20 March 33AD at 8:08am

 B A Barabbas Quit your jibba-jabba, you crazy fool!
🕐 Friday 20 March 33AD at 8:09am

 Hannibal No, Mad Dog might be on to something. I'll print some leaflets advertising a free out-of-town Passover concert featuring The Zebedees. That'll get Jesus's supporters out of the way.
🕐 Friday 20 March 33AD at 8:11am

 The Face And I'll poke all the girls in my address book and tell them to come to a "Free Barabbas" party outside the palace.
🕐 Friday 20 March 33AD at 8:13am

 Hannibal I'll disguise myself as The Zebedees, so that no-one realises they've been duped.
🕐 Friday 20 March 33AD at 8:15am

 Mad Dog Hannibal is on the jazz!
🕐 Friday 20 March 33AD at 8:16am

 B A Barabbas Poor Jesus! I pity the fool!
🕐 Friday 20 March 33AD at 8:18am

Hannibal I love it when a plan comes together!
🕐 Friday 20 March 33AD at 8:20am

Loggeth out

Friends
B A Barabbas hath 4 friends
See all
Find more friends

 Colonel Hannibal
 Mad Dog
 The Face
 Humpy Pumpy

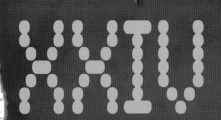

XXIV

The following takes place between 3:00pm 19 March and 3:00pm 20 March 33AD. My name is Jesus of Nazareth and this is the longest day of my life...

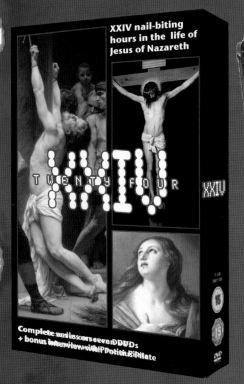

XXIV nail-biting hours in the life of Jesus of Nazareth

Complete series across seven DVDs + bonus interview with Pontius Pilate

DISC TWO

3:00 A.M. – 4:00 A.M.
Simon Zelotes is arrested, accused of being a terrorist. Jesus is taken and brought to trial.

4:00 A.M. – 5:00 A.M.
Jesus is tortured by Caiaphas. Meanwhile, Simon Peter denies any links with Jesus.

5:00 A.M. – 6:00 A.M.
Jesus is beaten and mocked as Simon Zelotes is condemned by Pontius Pilate.

6:00 A.M. – 7:00 A.M.
Herod Antipas offers a bribe for the release of Barabbas as Judas Iscariot disappears.

DISC THREE

7:00 A.M. – 8:00 A.M.
Pilate puts on a public charade to release Barabbas. Herod Agrippa tortures Jesus.

8:00 A.M. – 9:00 A.M.
Jesus is condemned by Pilate and is sent for crucifiction. Jesus refuses poison.

9:00 A.M. – 10:00 A.M.
The crosses are erected while John Mark chooses a new pair of shoes.

10:00 A.M. – 11:00 A.M.
As Jesus is taken for crucifiction, Pilate receives intelligence that a nuclear device has been planted somewhere in Jerusalem.

"THE MOST **PASSIONATE**, EXPLOSIVE AND **PUNISHINGLY BRUTAL** DRAMA TO BE SEEN ANYWHERE SINCE **AT HOME WITH THE CAESARS**"

Pontius Pilate

 Pontius Pilate Well, well. Who'd have thought the mob would vote to free Barabbas instead of their 'King of the Jews'? Still, that's the last we'll hear of Jesus.
⏱ Friday 20 March 33AD at 9:10am • Saith • Liketh

 Joseph ben Caiaphas Excellent day's work, Pontius! Jesus crucified, and hardly a hint of a riot. We're thinking of renaming today 'Good Friday'. What d'you think?
⏱ Friday 20 March 33AD at 2:28pm • Saith • Liketh

 Pontius Pilate Yes, apart from the hours of preternatural darkness and the violent earthquake that accompanied the crucifixion, today's been a corker.
⏱ Friday 20 March 33AD at 2:31pm

 Joseph of Arimathea Pilate, now Jesus is dead, I wonder if Nicodemus and I might be allowed to take down his body to protect it from souvenir hunters? There's a sicko demand for anything to do with Jesus – bottles of Cana wine are fetching a talent on theeBay.
⏱ Friday 20 March 33AD at 4:01pm • Saith • Liketh

 Pontius Pilate Dead? He's only been up there a few hours. Even a Spaniard will last a day!
⏱ Friday 20 March 33AD at 4:12pm

 Joseph of Arimathea He gave up the ghost over an hour ago. I can send you 200 talents in proof if you like.
⏱ Friday 20 March 33AD at 4:13pm

 Pontius Pilate Sold! But leave a discreet interval before you start selling his body parts, eh?
⏱ Friday 20 March 33AD at 4:14pm

View Mine Icons (36)

Edit Mine Profile

Roman Governor of Judea

Personal Information

Birthday	Status
25 June	**Married to Claudia Procula**
Website:	
www.governorofjudea.gov.rm	

Proclamations

Miss the roar and the crowd?

Full satellite coverage of all major Colosseum events for just 120sh.

👍 Liketh 🖐 Despiseth

Become a Jew today!

2-for-1 until the end of March!

👍 Liketh 🖐 Despiseth

Loggeth out

Friends
Pontius Pilate hath 316 friends
See all
Find more friends

 Herod Antipas

 Naevius Macro

 Annas ben Seth

Herod Philip

theEbaY

jesus of nazareth_ | All Categories | **Searcheth**

Home > Buyeth > **Search results for "jesus of nazareth"**

| **All items** | **Auction only** | **Buyeth now!** |

Description		Price	Time left
Genuine urns of wine from the Marriage at Cana. Red and white available. Beautifully presented.	104 bids	**1500shek**	1hr 20min
VERY UNIQUE. 3x2in blocks of wood from the ONE TRUE CROSS. 10,000 available.	Buyeth now	**120shek**	3hr 51min
Nails from the cross of the Messiah. Four available.	3507 bids	**33shek**	7hr 13min
GENUINE signed icon of Jesus on the cross. "To John, Love Jesus xxx". One only.	Buyeth now	**1250shek**	7hr 15min

Mary Magdalene

 Mary Magdalene OMG!! You won't believe this! The Virgin Mary and I just went to Jesus's sepulchre. His body was gone and there were two angels sitting there!
⏱ Sunday 22 March 33AD at 5:15am • Saith • Liketh

 Doubting Thomas Why wouldn't we believe that? I saw them myself – they were riding on the back of a unicorn singing "It's a long way to Tipperary!" lol!
⏱ Sunday 22 March 33AD at 5:17am

 Virgin Mary I know angels when I see them, young man. I once met the Archangel Gabriel, you know! He said I was going to have a son by the Holy Ghost and I should call him Emmanuel. But Joseph said that was a girl's name, and a bit slutty, so we settled on Jesus.
⏱ Sunday 22 March 33AD at 5:21am

 Mary Magdalene The angels said he'd risen from the dead!
⏱ Sunday 22 March 33AD at 5:23am

 Simon Peter I think you've both been on the sauce!
⏱ Sunday 22 March 33AD at 5:25am

 Mary Magdalene Once, twice, three times. That's a lie!
⏱ Sunday 22 March 33AD at 5:26am

 Simon Peter All right, leave it out.
⏱ Sunday 22 March 33AD at 5:26am

 Mary Magdalene They also said, "remember how Jesus spake unto you, saying, 'the Son of Man must be delivered into the hands of sinful men, and be crucified, and on the third day rise again'."
⏱ Sunday 22 March 33AD at 5:28am

 Jude Thaddeus But he was always saying shit like that.
⏱ Sunday 22 March 33AD at 5:29am

 Jesus Christ Da-nah! O ye fools, that are slow to believe the words of the prophets! I'm back!
⏱ Sunday 22 March 33AD at 3:01pm • Saith • Liketh

 Doubting Thomas Whoever you are, that's a pretty sick joke. Loggeth out now!
⏱ Sunday 22 March 33AD at 3:03pm

 John Zebedee No, no, dude, that's definitely Jesus!
⏱ Sunday 22 March 33AD at 3:04pm

View Mine Icons (464)

Edit Mine Profile

Jesus loved me best!

Personal Information

Birthday
22 July

Status
It's extremely complicated

Website:
www.ilovejesus.jd

Proclamations

Child on the way?

In the event it's a boy, let us arrange a sumptuous banquet to celebrate the birth. Call today!

👍 Liketh 💬 Despiseth

Ritually unclean woman?

You gave birth to original sin, but that's no need to stink. Why not join our friendly spa today?

👍 Liketh 💬 Despiseth

Loggeth out

Friends
Mary Magdalene hath 13554 friends
See all
Find more friends

 Virgin Mary   Ol' Ma Zebedee   Suzanna Myrbarer   Martha Magdalene

Going up!

Post Card

Celestial Mail Service
Patron: Archangel Gabriel

Hi guys,

Hope you're well. Heaven is great – the manna is excellent. No tummy troubles at all! Honestly, Thomas! Hope you're all behaving yourselves (John Zebedee!!!). You might run into some trouble with a bloke named Paul, but, don't worry, I'll have a word. Don't let him bully you!

Peace and love.

The Saviour!

The Apostles c/o Simon Peter

The Ugly Farm (kidding!)

Capernaum, Galilee

THY-FACE.COM

Simon Peter

 Jesus Christ Peter, do you love me?
🕛 Thursday 30 April 33AD at 7:00am • Saith • Liketh

 Simon Peter Yes, you know I do.
🕛 Thursday 30 April 33AD at 7:01am

 Jesus Christ Then feed my lambs.
🕛 Thursday 30 April 33AD at 7:02am

 Jesus Christ Peter, do you love me?
🕛 Thursday 30 April 33AD at 8:00am • Saith • Liketh

 Simon Peter Yes, you know I do.
🕛 Thursday 30 April 33AD at 8:04am

 Jesus Christ Then feed my sheep.
🕛 Thursday 30 April 33AD at 8:05am

 Jesus Christ Peter, do you love me?
🕛 Thursday 30 April 33AD at 9:00am • Saith • Liketh

 Simon Peter Christ! I'll feed your bleedin hippopotamus, yes. I thought you were leaving soon?
🕛 Thursday 30 April 33AD at 9:06am

 Jesus Christ I am! I hath been risen 40 days. Now is the time for me to ascend to Heaven.
🕛 Thursday 30 April 33AD at 9:07am

 Simon Zelotes Aren't you going to restore the Kingdom of Israel? I thought that was the point.
🕛 Thursday 30 April 33AD at 9:08am

 Jesus Christ It is not for you to know God's timetable. Now go into the world and preach the gospel: be nice to people and forgive all transgressions. Treat others as you would have them treat you; forego money and material wealth and create a world filled with peace and love.
🕛 Thursday 30 April 33AD at 9:09am

 John Zebedee Yes, yes, we get it! Say hi to your dads from us, and don't be a stranger!
🕛 Thursday 30 April 33AD at 9:10am

 Jesus Christ Farewell. And remember. I'll be back.
🕛 Thursday 30 April 33AD at 9:11am

HATH COME TO PASS

👋 Jesus Christ's ThyFace account hath been Suspended • Saith • Liketh

Loggeth out

View Mine Icons (1)

Edit Mine Profile

"The Rock"

Personal Information

Birthday	Status
29 June 1BC	**Widowed :-)**

Website:
www.iamarock.gal

Proclamations

We're partying tonight!

Why not join us online?

👍 Liketh 👎 Despiseth

Pro-wrestling takes guts

And our guys definitely have guts. Book your tickets now!

👍 Liketh 👎 Despiseth

Friends
Simon Peter hath 254 friends
See all
Find more friends

 Andrew the Fish   Jesus Christ   John Zebedee   James Zebedee

APPLICATION FOR THE POST OF
APOSTLE OF JESUS

PLEASE ANSWER ALL QUESTIONS
TO THE BEST OF YOUR ABILITY

1 Name *Saul aka Paul*   2 Place of birth *Tarsus*

3 Ethnic background *Jewish*   4 Nationality *Roman citizen*

5 Date of birth *29 June 10AD*   6 Sex *Against it*

---

7 Education *Educated in Pharisee theology in Jerusalem as pupil of Chief Pharisee Gamaliel ben Simeon.*

---

8 Current employment *Persecutor of minority religions*

---

9 Hobbies *Tent making, attending stonings and golf*

---

10 Theological viewpoint

See attached 13 epistles, but I feel that as long as Christianity is limited to Jews it will always remain a ghetto religion. I believe if it were extended to include gentiles, it has the potential to be one of the biggies, possibly even bigger than the Graeco-Roman pantheon itself. Of course, if we wanted to aim that high, we'd need to change the rules to let men keep their dicks intact.

---

11 Current salary *550 shekels pcm + healing insurance*

PTO

THY-FACE.COM

James Zebedee

 James Zebedee I can't remember where we hid the scrolls. Anyone know what we're supposed to be doing?
🕐 Friday 1 May 33AD at 5:30pm • Saith • Liketh

 John Mark It definitely had something to do with hating homos. We really hate them, don't we?
🕐 Friday 1 May 33AD at 5:32pm

 Apostle Philip And liberals. Don't forget liberals.
🕐 Friday 1 May 33AD at 5:35pm

 Andrew the Fish And one day a week you have to eat fish.
🕐 Friday 1 May 33AD at 5:37pm

 Doubting Thomas Yeah right. And a chocolate egg to celebrate Jesus's resurrection! lol!
🕐 Friday 1 May 33AD at 5:38pm

 Mary Magdalene There was also a bunch of stuff about socialised medicine.
🕐 Friday 1 May 33AD at 5:55pm

 Jude Thaddeus Hey, women don't get a say! Shouldn't you be at home looking after the baby?
🕐 Friday 1 May 33AD at 5:56pm

 Matthew Levi I seem to recall the principal aim being to make as much money as possible.
🕐 Friday 1 May 33AD at 5:39pm

 Simon Peter And converting everyone in the whole world to our religion! Hey – bagsy me be Pope!
🕐 Friday 1 May 33AD at 5:42pm

James the Less And we can all wear little crucifixes!
🕐 Friday 1 May 33AD at 5:45pm

James Zebedee That is way too sick, dude! So how do we go about converting the whole world?
🕐 Friday 1 May 33AD at 5:47pm

Simon Zelotes By smiting all the unbelievers!
🕐 Friday 1 May 33AD at 5:49pm

 John Zebedee Right then, that's the next bunch of centuries sorted! Let's do some good!
🕐 Friday 1 May 33AD at 5:59pm

James Zebedee Amen to that!
🕐 Friday 1 May 33AD at 6:00pm

View Mine Icons (58)

Edit Mine Profile

The Talented One

Personal Information

Birthday
25 July

Status
Casual dude

Website:
www.planetzebedee.com

Proclamations

Jesus jello moulds

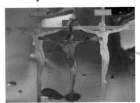

Perfect with bread and wine.

👍 Liketh 👎 Despiseth

Situations vacant: Apostle

We are looking for a 12th apostle to join our busy team. No lefties.

👍 Liketh 👎 Despiseth

Loggeth out

Friends
James Zebedee hath 16643 friends
See all
Find more friends

 Herod Agrippa

 Jesus Junior

 Simon Peter

 John Zebedee

THE ACTS OF THE APOSTLES (ABRIDGED)

Judas Iscariot After Simon Zelotes found Judas hanging from a tree, he tried to save him, but accidentally disembowelled him with his sword.

Simon Zelotes Formed a magic act under the name of Simon Magus and accidentally sawed himself in half during a stage show in Persia.

Apostle Philip Preached in Greece with a cheeky ventriloquist goat. After the goat insulted the proconsul's wife, both Philip and the goat were crucified.

Doubting Thomas Founded the Order of Sceptics, but refused to join. Died in Rome in 64AD after deciding a shout of "fire!" was someone joking.

Matthew Levi Wrote the popular Gospel of Saint Matthew and the somewhat less popular "Matthew's Guide to Double-Entry Bookkeeping".

Andrew the Fish Opened fish shops in Russia, Romania, Greece, Portugal and Scotland. Crucified in Scotland for not selling chips.

Jude Thaddeus Spent his life trying to bring peace to the Middle East. Martyred in Beirut before becoming the Saint of Lost Causes.

John Mark Launched a successful range of haircare products. Preached the Word of God and continued to put it about among his loyal clientele.

James the Less Stoned to death on the order of High Priest Annas ben Annas in 64AD after misspelling his name once too often.

James Zebedee Quit The Zebedees citing musical differences: "John's like completely mental." Became a DJ on the Spanish clubbing circuit.

Simon Peter First Pope in Rome. Crucified upside down by Emperor Nero, who wanted to see if he was any better looking the other way up.

John Zebedee Wrote the Revelation of St John. With his book and music royalties built the Zebedee Mansion, where he died in his bed aged 94.

If you enjoyed
Jesus on ThyFace
you might enjoy one of
these other books
in the series…

Jesus on ThyFace 2

The Second Coming of the Messiah

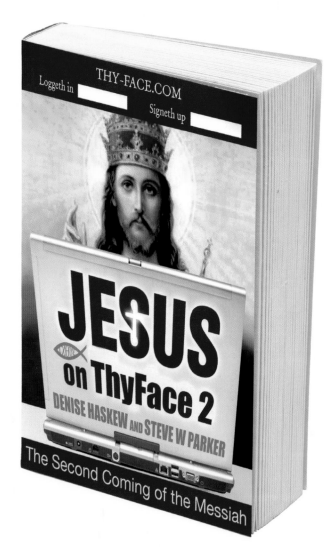

Date to be confirmed

Mohammad
A Life in Pictures

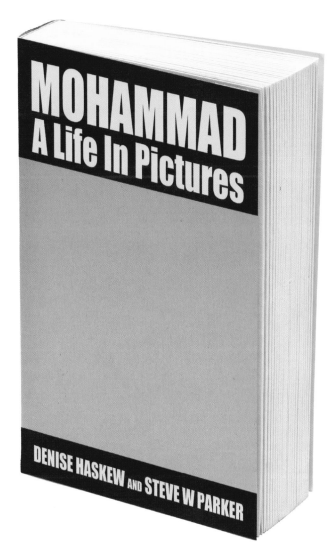

Braille version available

God on ThyFace

Social Networking for the Modern Deity

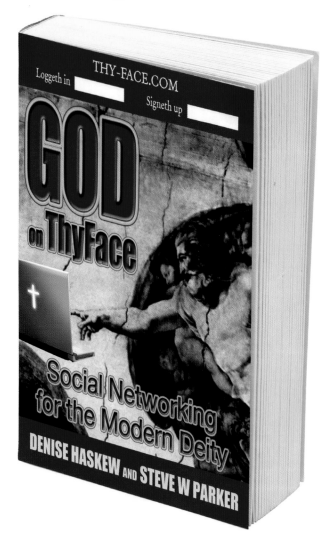

Parental warning:
Contains fornication, smiting and mild cursing

Keep Fit With Buddha

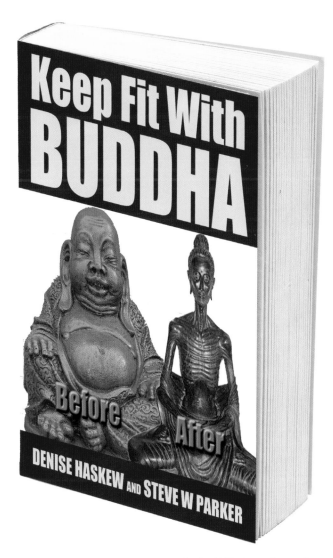

Enlighten your midriff today!

Acts of the Apostles

The Further Adventures of the Twelve Stooges

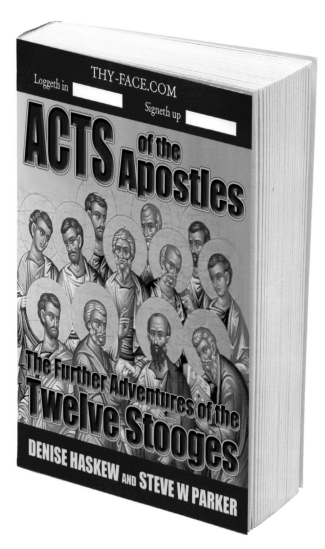

Including "Epistles" and the shocking "Revelation of St John Zebedee"